Ecstasy

By Samuel Shuford Snodgrass

Mankind has a blessing in woman's beauty. Every woman's body has a beauty as nature created in it. Her torso has a romantic appeal, creates desire and lust, and has an allure that attracts and holds the envious eyes of men. Glamour may or may not be a part of this depending on the proportions and textures the woman has. The female body has moistness, freshness, softness, graceful curvatures, and warmth. She is man's amorous partner. She becomes a mother by giving birth. Her hips hold new life. Her breasts produce nourishing milk for the newborn. She is a passive creature of art. She was created for the nurturant purposes of humanity. Face, arms, hands, legs, and feet elicit a unique dainty loveliness. I have attempted to portray her in an appealing set of paintings for my readers' enjoyment and pleasure. Each woman is a gracious goddess that spellbounds the viewer with her attractiveness.

The objective of this book is to artistically express a display of the beauty of women. Any woman. Beauty. Adorable beauty.

Some reclining nude female paintings have the appearance of a still life of a bowl of fruit, especially of pears. Standing female nudes somewhat resemble a multi-shaped flower vase. A woman's image warms a man's heart. He desires to have her attentions and caress her affectionately. She is the most romantic form of art objects. There is an inherent beauty to her that is found nowhere else. As time has marked out the centuries, numerous famous talented masters of painting have painted nude females. She is a most popular and frequent subject for art. She is akin to a flower with a soft delicate loveliness that the human eye enjoys completely.

Beauty of women has been exploited by the fashion industry, cosmetics, the movie business, jewelry, woman's fashion and glamour magazines, advertizing industry, modeling, the dancing arts, strip clubs, pornography, the theater, art and artists, sculptors, furs, and perfumes.

Innocence, desire, purity. A female is like a streamlined bird, swan, flower, fish, car, airplane, ship, sleek greyhound, jaguar, or a graceful horse in motion. A female has much natural beauty. Priestess, aesthetic, perfection, a gorgeous goddess of glamour. Dainty, delicate features.

She is both classical art and modern art. She definitely has that sparkle.
Beauty is glamour, enchantment, and magic. Beauty or charm is that which is romantically attractive. It is the attractive or exciting quality that makes certain people seem appealing or special. Beauty is a combination of qualities such as shape, color, or form that pleases the aesthetic senses, especially the sight.

There are many different kinds of beauty.

A woman at any age has beauty.

Beauty comes from shape, color, and form that please the aesthetic sense.

A woman's sensuous glamorous beauty is the gracious art of nature.

Beauty:
Allure, grace, bloom, glamour, symmetry, artistry, refinement, class, handsome, winsome, charm, style, comeliness, delicacy, adorableness, exquisite, polish, elegance, allurement, pulchritude, good looks, attractive, fascination, shapeliness, angelic, appeal. Dazzling darlings of delight.

She has the balance of nature.
She is the balance of nature.
Why is she so beautiful?
Symmetry and proportion are a part of why this is so.
Hair, face, paired features on the sides on a mid line, top, bottom, left, right.
Paired eyes, ears, nostrils, breasts, arms, legs, hands, feet, fingers, buttocks, toes, and shoulder blades.
Single nose, mouth, navel, backbone line, pubic cleft.

The artwork presented has a process of creation. First there is an idea. It is sketched in a spiral notebook. Setting in a lounge recliner rocking chair, I drink black coffee, eat peppermints, smoke a pipe and tobacco, listen to the radio, and have daylight from a window on my drawing page. A pencil is used. A clip board or a piece of smooth Masonite is my drawing surface held in my lap. Usually it is freehand sketched. A ruler may used to get things closely right, symmetric, or spaced exactly. A small blank piece of paper may also be used on which tic mark measurements are placed to arrange the drawing. The drawing may be redrawn. Mistakes are erased and redone. Lengths, curves, and shapes need reworking sometimes. The page is divided into numerous datum lines with a ruler to space out the drawing accurately. Or it may be just drawn unassisted. The work piece is seat aside for a time. Later it is reexamined to see what was done earlier and a decision is made if it needs more work. It may be redrawn. Pencil work is correctable. When certain of a final work piece, it is redrawn with a black felt tip marker. All pencil marks are erased. Then the figure is water colored until the figure until it is right.

The Body Components:
Head: face, hair, ears, eyes, brows, lashes, eye sockets, nose, cheeks, forehead, temples, lips, teeth, jaw, and chin
Neck
Shoulders
Upper arms
Elbows
Fore arms
Wrists
Hands: thumb, fingers, palm, and the back of the hand
Back
Chest

Breasts
Waist
Hips
Buttocks
Crotch
Thighs
Knees
Calves
Ankles
Feet: heels, soles, toes, and the body of the foot

Art Materials:
Brush: number 3, Chinese, sable. It is broken it in by repeatedly putting water on it and brushing it on a white cotton tee shirt rag.
Masonite board to paint on: I set in a Lazy Boy recliner chair with this board in my lap, near a bay window that has nice natural daylight. It is on the house's east side. Painting times are only mornings from 8:00 to about 1:00. The light is soft and even.
Water: is put in a Styrofoam egg carton.
White cotton tee shirt rags, Q tips, and my finger tips are used to clean up paint that has gone past the felt tip figure lines or when too much water and paint is placed on my paper.
Watercolor Paper: 9 inches x 12 inches that is cut to 8.5 inches x 11 inches. Cold press, student grade, light weight, 90 lb, acid and lignin free. Canson Montval, CPP, Strathmore 200 series, good, U Create watercolor paper brands.
Spiral ringed notebooks with blue college ruled lines for preliminary pencil sketches.
Paint: Crayola washable, watercolors, 8 colors. Prang washable semi moist watercolors, 8 colors, Dixon.
Pencils: Papermate number 2.
Pink Pearl erasers.
Sharpie ultra fine point permanent black felt tip marker and colored ones too.

The Process:
The watercolor paper is at first all plain with nothing on it. In a spiral ringed notebook the figures are sketched with pencil. Next erase and redraw as desired. Then the figure is redrawn on watercolor paper with pencil. Datum construction horizontal or vertical lines on the first notebook sketch may be made to help transfer it accurately to the watercolor paper. Then carefully black felt tip pen traces are made over the pencil lines on the watercolor paper. The brush is wet with water, shook down to the floor to straighten the hairs, and put into the color cake of paint. More water is put on the cake with the brush and swirled about to make a loose pool of paint. Some paint is picked up with the brush and put it on the watercolor paper. The color is too dark. So it is spread out with the brush and gets lighter. Too much water put on the paper will cause it to run, separate into light and dark areas, and wrinkle the paper. The excess is tee shirt cloth or Q tip removed. Borders are not outlined as this stays and can be seen. This ruins the drawing.

Color is added and moved around. White areas or lighter spaces of color are left to make the figure fill out appropriately. The color dry is allowed to dry for three to six hours before more is added. This prevents run over of different colors. The same area may be painted several times (washes) to darken and enrich the texture of the color. Small delicate and hard to reach colored areas like eyes, eyelids, lips, feet, toes, hands, and fingers, may be colored with watercolors or colored felt tip pen. The hair, face, limbs, torso, hands, and feet are drawn differently in each drawing as what works for one will not work for others. Each is unique. Some are realistic. Some look like classical subjects painted by the masters centuries ago. Others are cartoon characters. Some look like people I know. Others are skinny beauties like tall thin actresses and models. Models are tall, slender, and beautiful. All beautiful women are not slender and tall. Some look mid or full figured like classic statues or paintings of women by the masters. Others are not exact people but abstract people but abstract expression or impressions of women. Modern art. Distortion. Extreme. They resemble women in an unnatural creative way that is beyond nature and close to art.

Different body sizes, heights, faces, hair colors and styles, proportions, poses, and postures are used. Front, side, back, reclining, and standing drawings of women are included to add the spice of variety to this work.

A wide variety of female figures are portrayed. 78 subjects are included. Skin tone, texture, proportion, contour, bulk, and detail are very important. The idea is to portray beauty using different subjects, methods, and body types. Real women are like this. All women have a beauty of their own. Beauty is skin deep. Beauty is also inside, in the face, and eyes, poise, personality, behavior, soul, voice, manner, and actions of the figure. Beauty was a bull's eye aimed at 78 times. May the reader enjoy and appreciate this work.

Five hours is the usual work limit that I have for art work. Longer and stiffness, cramps, tired eyes, weary mind, and fatigue occurs. My ability and eagerness to perform are reduced. A fresh state the next day is best. Working too hard and long is counter productive.

With art, first there is nothing. You work with your materials until something begins to be created. You continue to completion.

The black and white piano keys scare some people. Others are attracted to them. Likewise, a blank white sheet of watercolor paper affects people different ways. It is a matter of attitude. A blank sheet may seem lonely and empty or a challenge to conquer.

You sketch a figure in pencil in a notebook and redraw it on the watercolor paper. Then you begin to have something. Construction lines are used with both vertical and horizontal datum lines and measures with tic marks on small bits of paper to assist the drawing transfer. The necessary change corrections are made until it is right. About a third of the time, drawings are thrown out and new different ones are made until I am completely satisfied. Ideas come easy and fast if given time to appear. A bad drawing seems to create a new better one.

Carefully the drawing is felt tip pen traced over the faint pencil marks to give a darker sharper clear bold image. The figure appears better and more realistically.

Coloring it in gives the figure reality, feeling, and a life likeness. The colors show shape and detail that is more pure art than just a sketched drawing. Different colors are best done with drying periods between painting to reduce smear and bleed over messes. It is best to use the least amount of water possible. Too much water gives dark and light areas with wrinkled, bubbled paper. Spreading out the colors well is the secret skill to using water colors effectively. People do this in different ways.

The figures appear with a plain white backdrop. No clothes, valance, jewelry, furs, hats, shoes, furniture, background objects, buildings, or landscapes, or colors. Just a single figure before a plain white background. The viewer's attention is focused on the figure better this way.

As children we painted watercolors. This was sometimes by number, in school, in store bought books at home. I can remember many Walt Disney books about his cartoon characters. These are educational, entertaining, and have a reward of their own that adds enrichment to anyone's childhood. It takes imagination, creativity, forethought, and ability to draw your own figures and then color them. But the two have about the same result: a finished work of art.

A woman has a beauty, glamour, attractiveness, gracefulness, and maybe elegance and seductiveness trait that the man lacks. Her graceful proportions, curves, shapes, bulges, and concavities give her a grace of line and form that appeals to the artistic taste. Nature made her so. Man looks at woman and appreciates her for this. The male idealizes his female as his romantic angelic goddess of love. He finds her fascinatingly attractive. A woman's life has a peaceful fragility that erupts in the grandeur of romance, marriage, and childbirth to create a family for her and her husband. She is the fruiting vine. The male and female are very different creatures but are a part of the same thing, humanity. They create love in the human world.

Love is ....
A flower in our lives.
So pure, delicate, and wise.
Without it
All is sad, empty, and bleak.
As we live
It is the lofty peak.
Without it we are lost, alone, and weak.
Love is ours now
Shinning on our brow.
Glowing hearts with joy.

A girl loves a boy.
Your pretty soft body
In my eyes
And in my hands
My feelings suddenly go hotly
And passion builds so grand.
If you be faithful
I will be so grateful.

Every woman is a goddess being of beauty can't be denied. Here now is a set of drawings for my audience's enjoyment and pleasure.

Here now is a book of art created about the female and her beauty. I hope the reader is contented with its contents.

The artist who is the beautician.

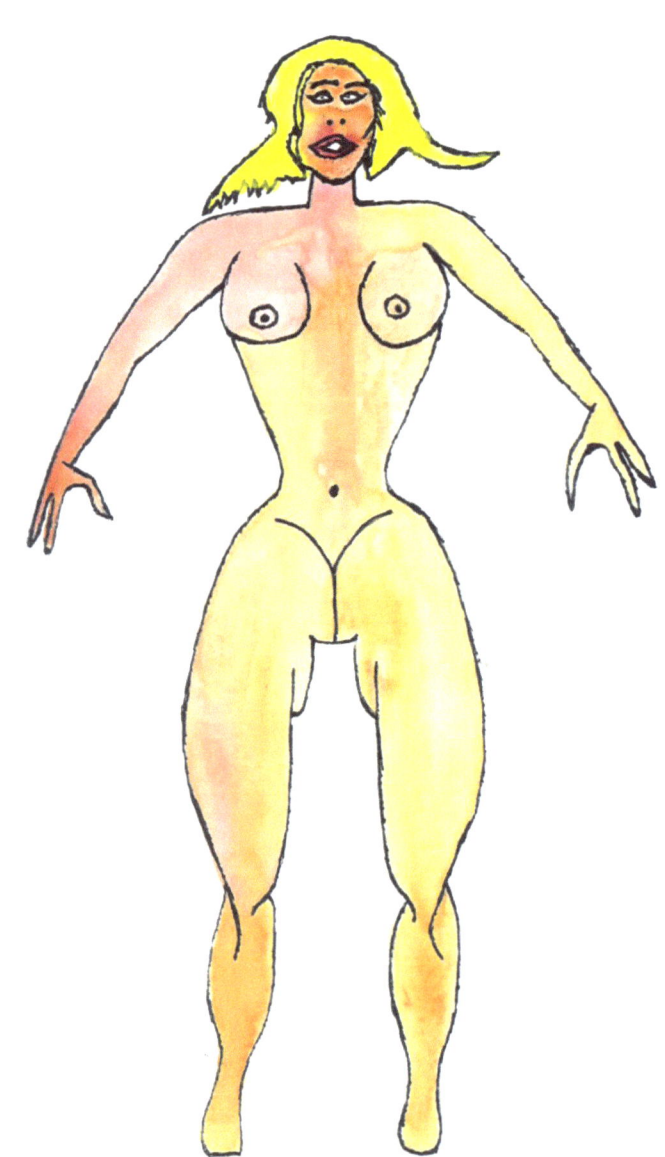

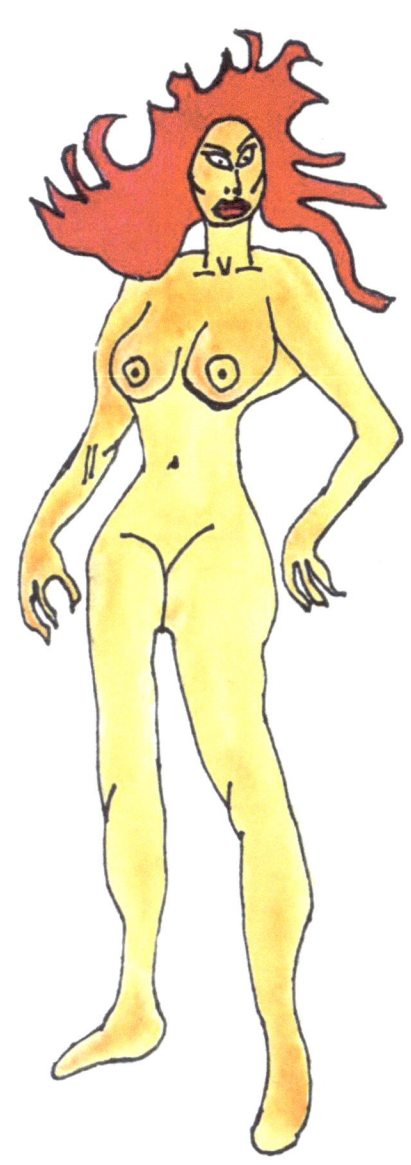

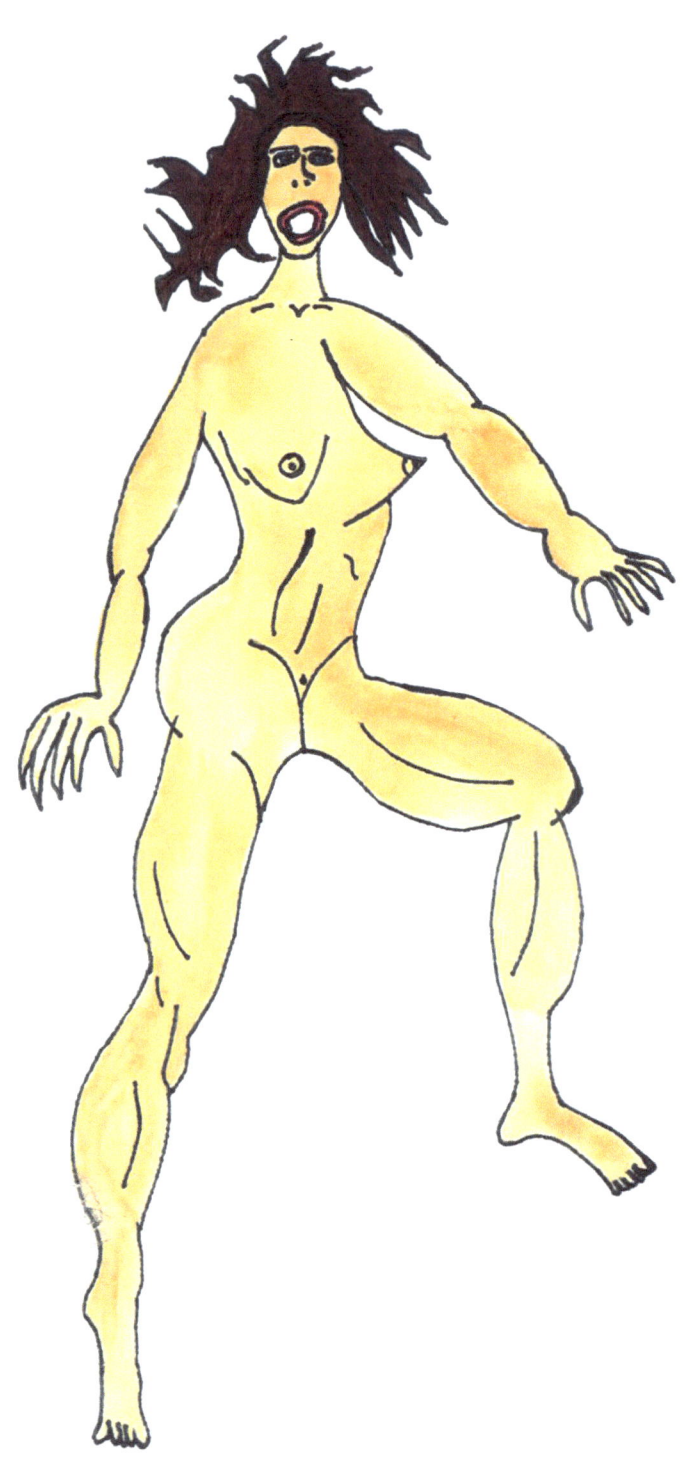

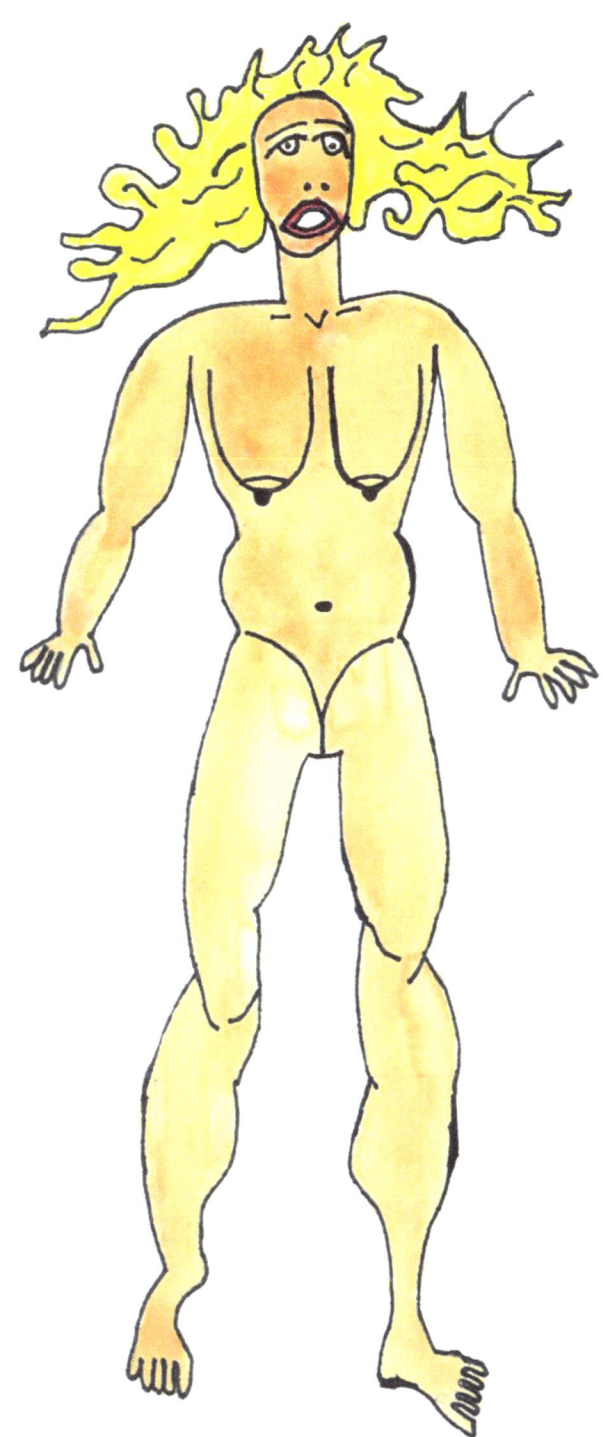

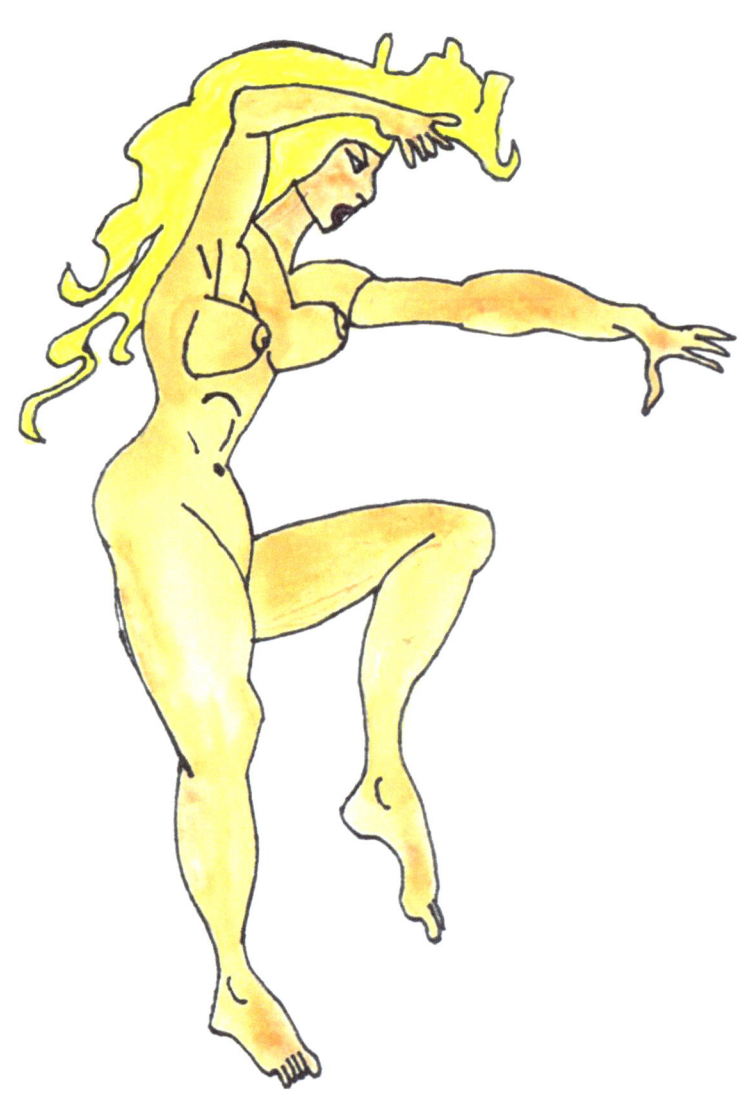

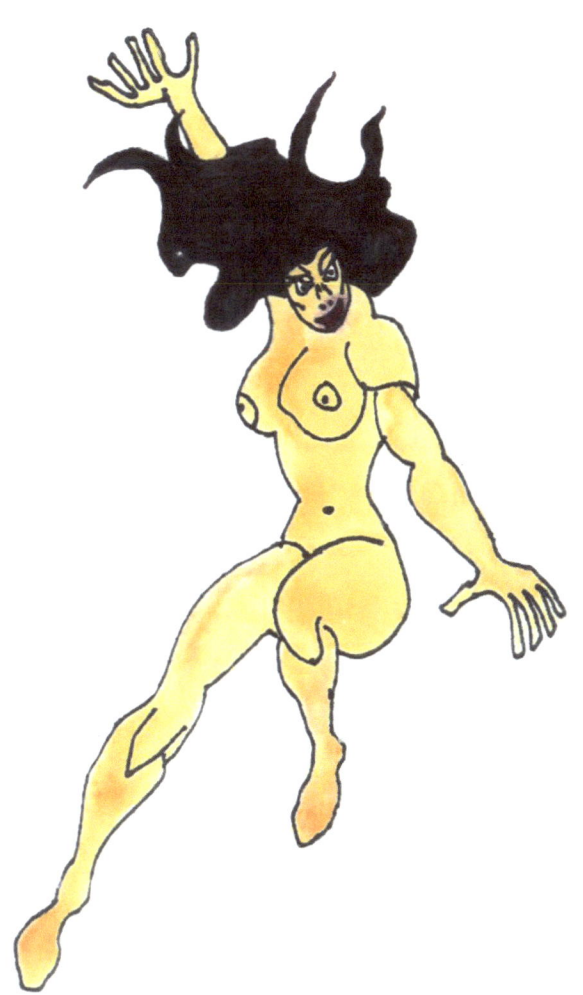

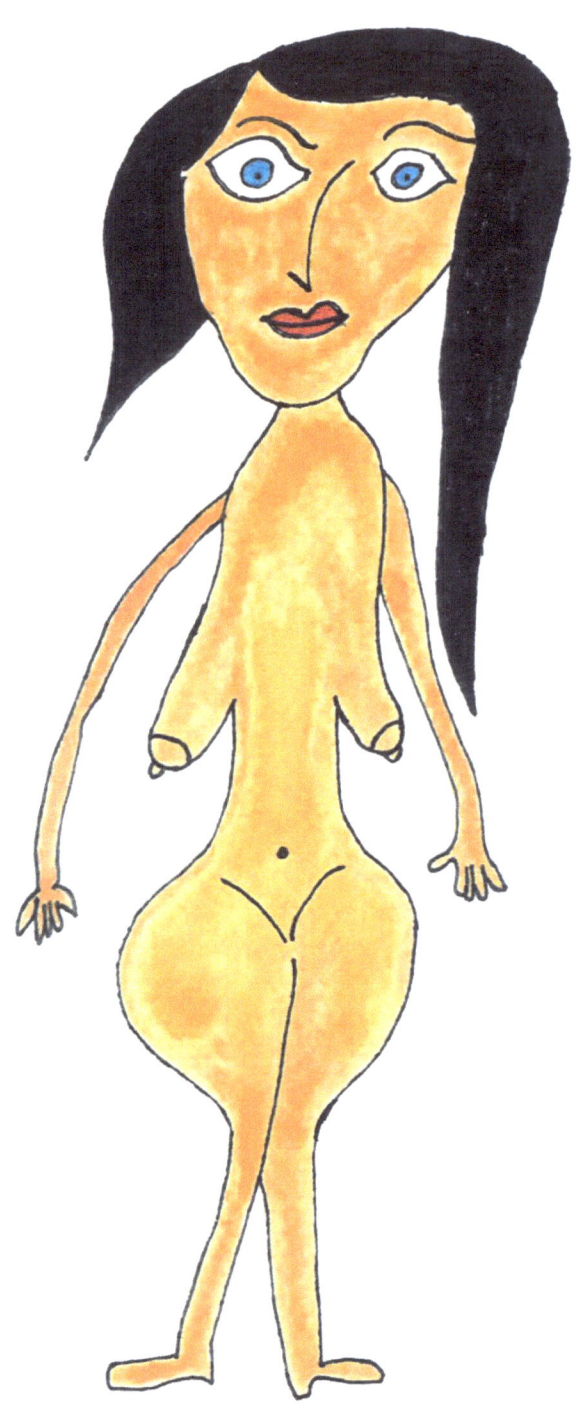

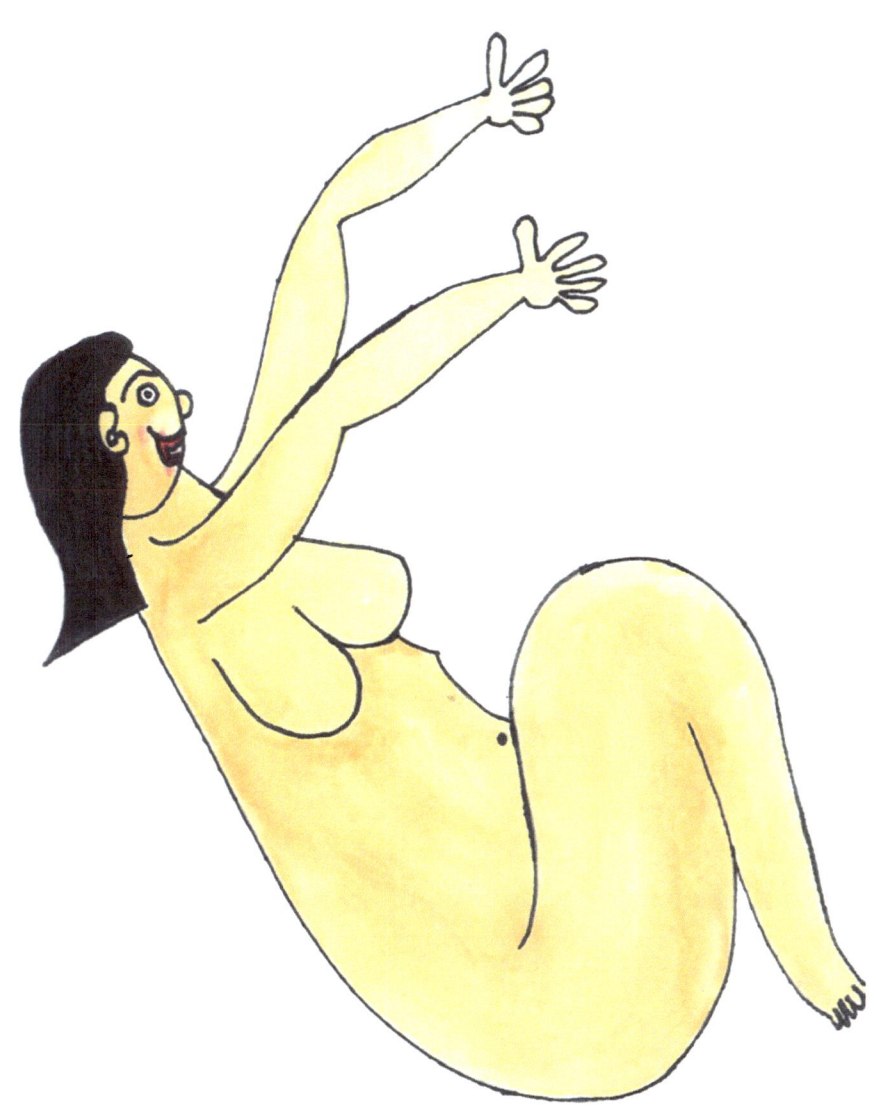

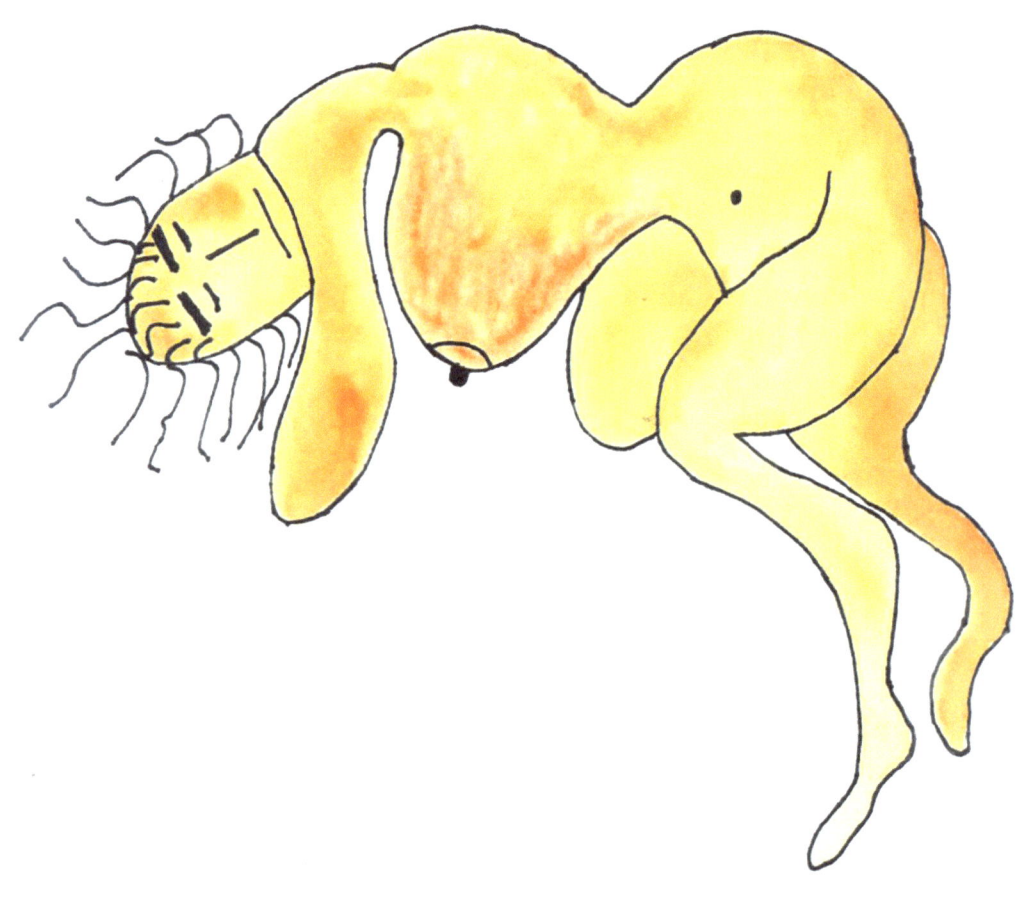

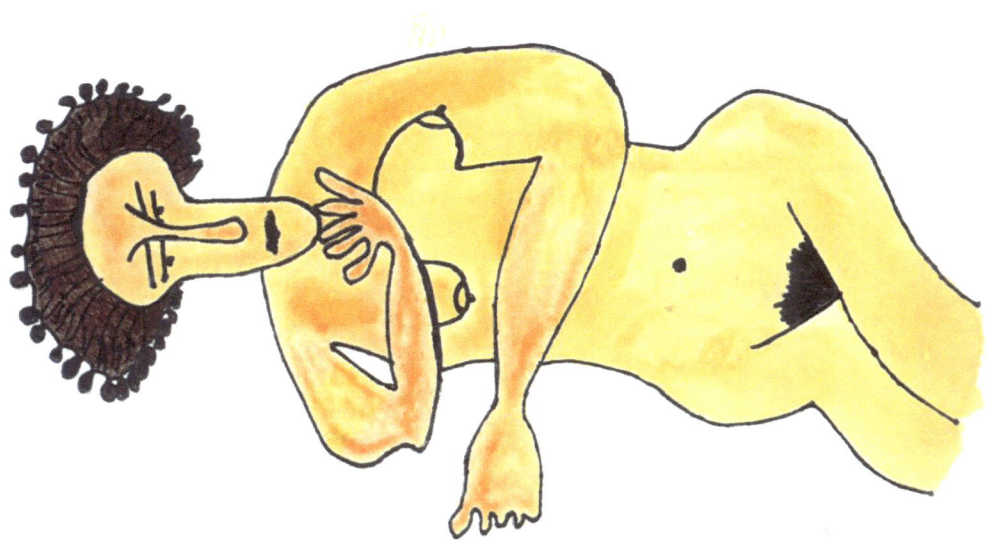

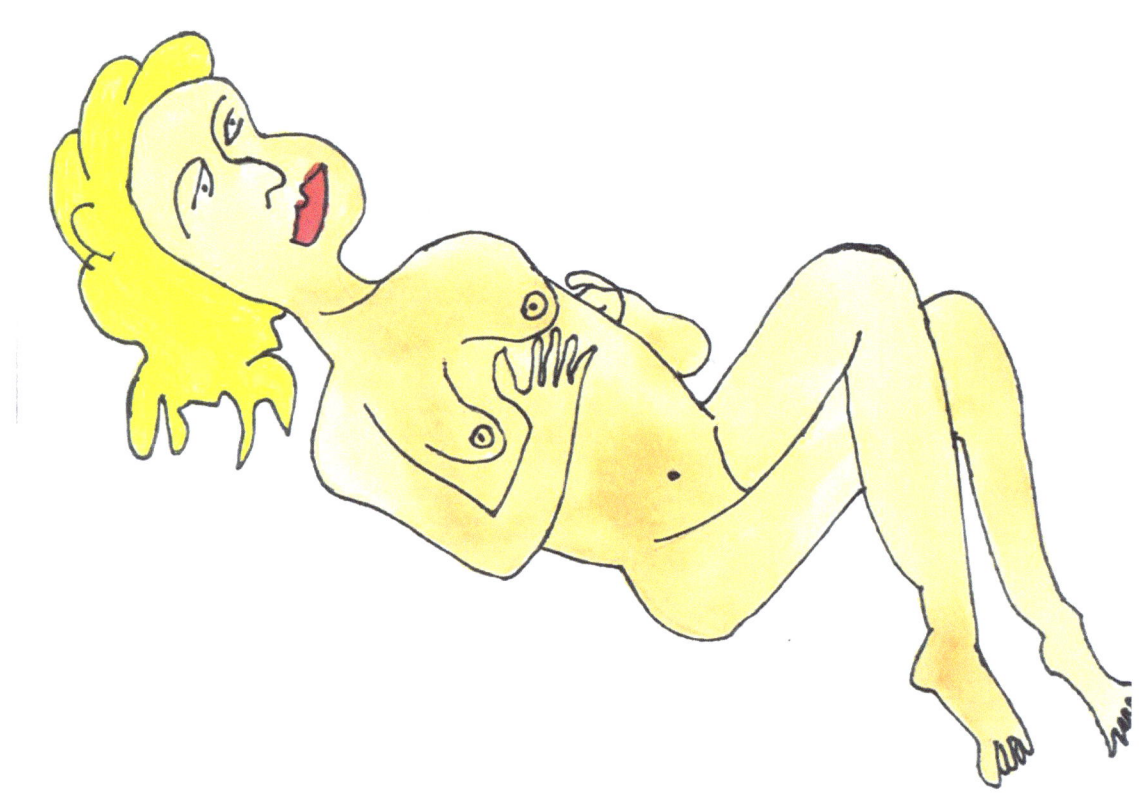

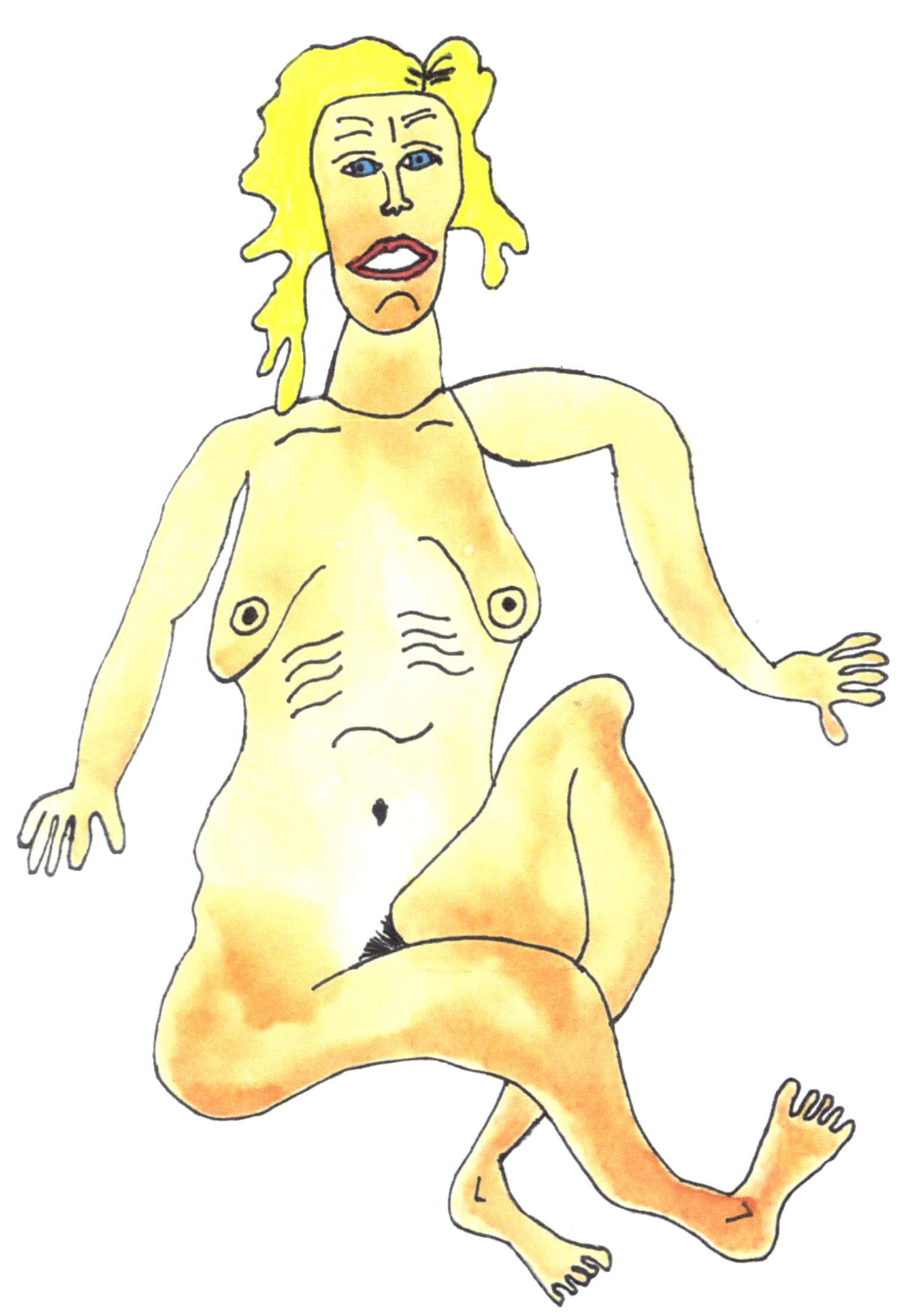

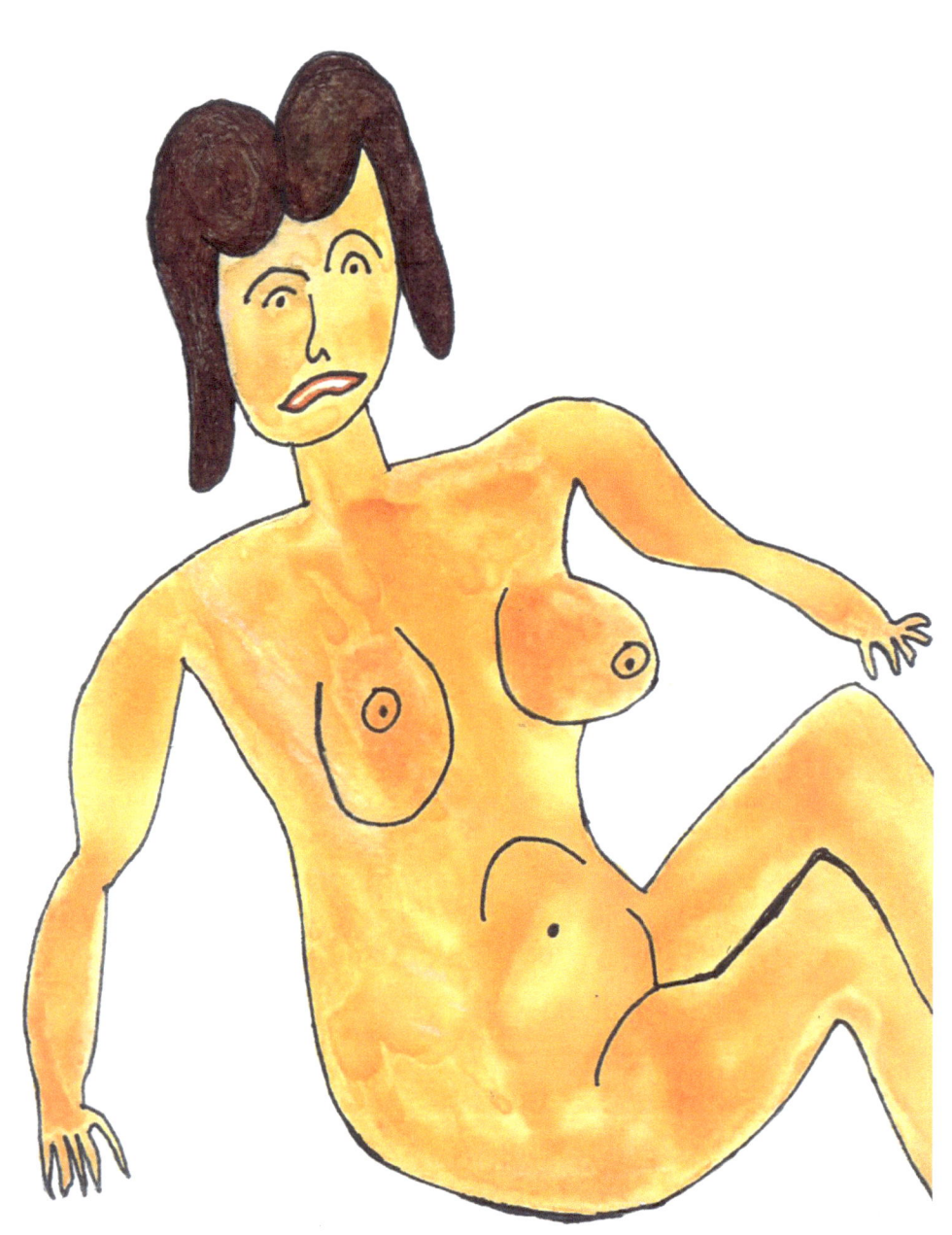

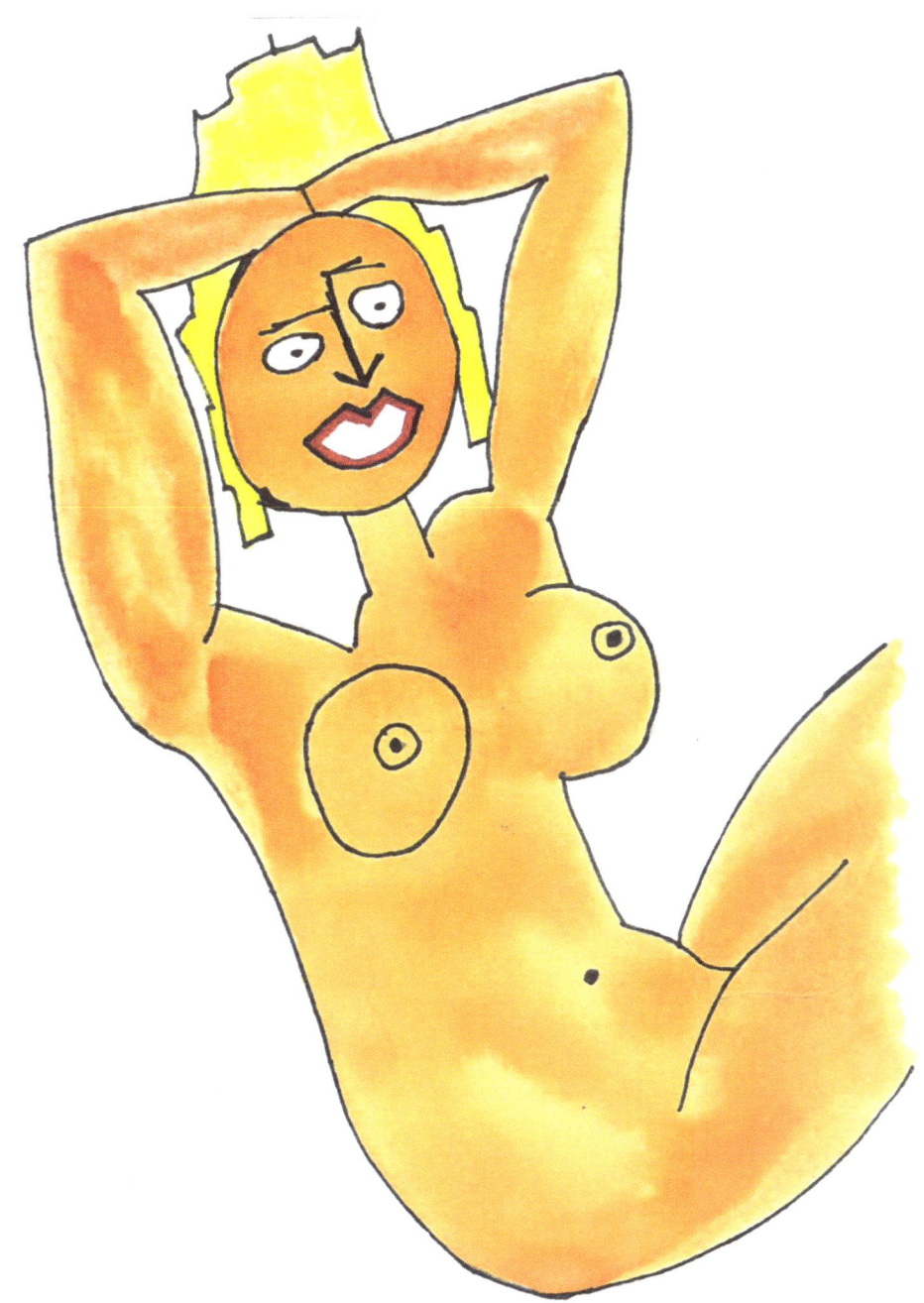

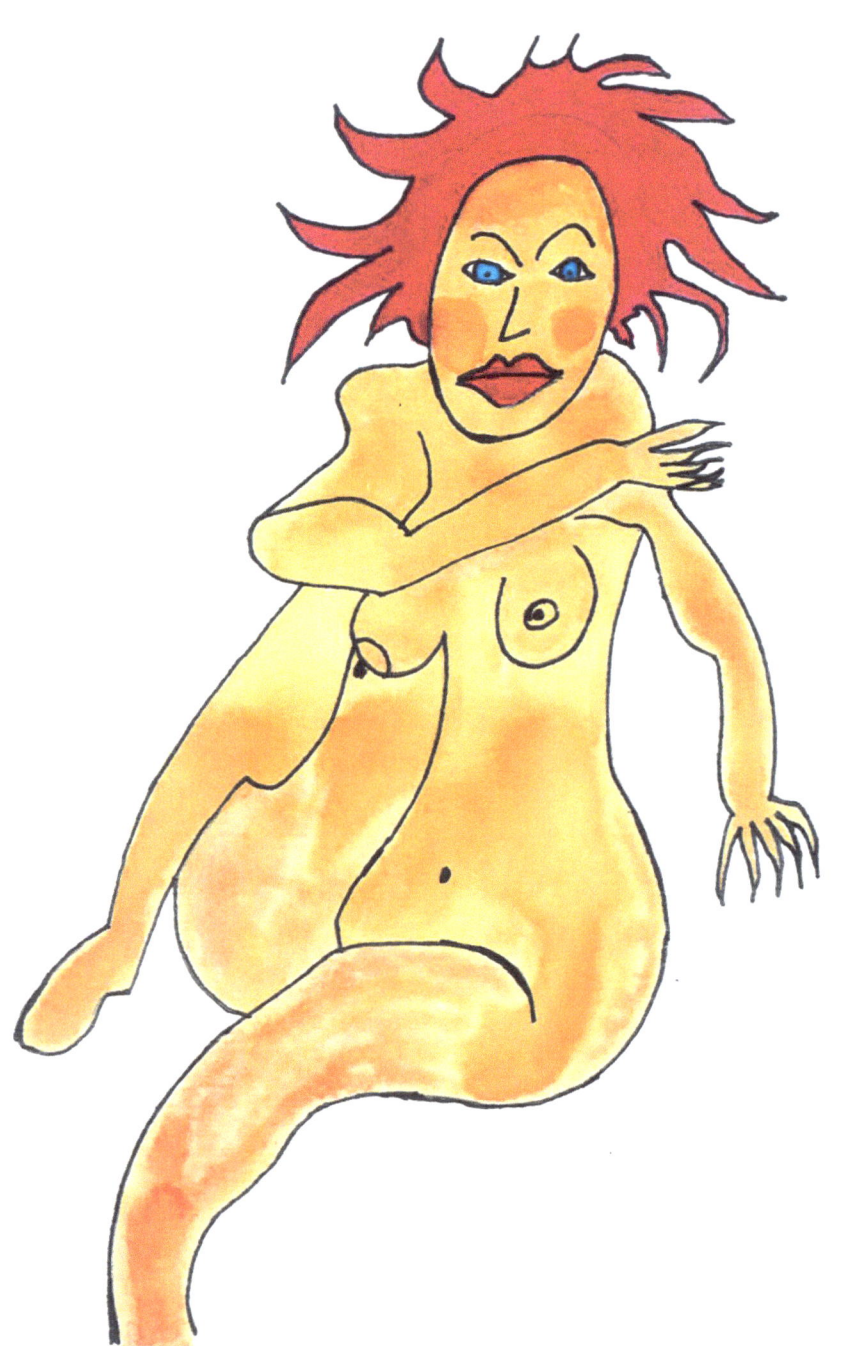

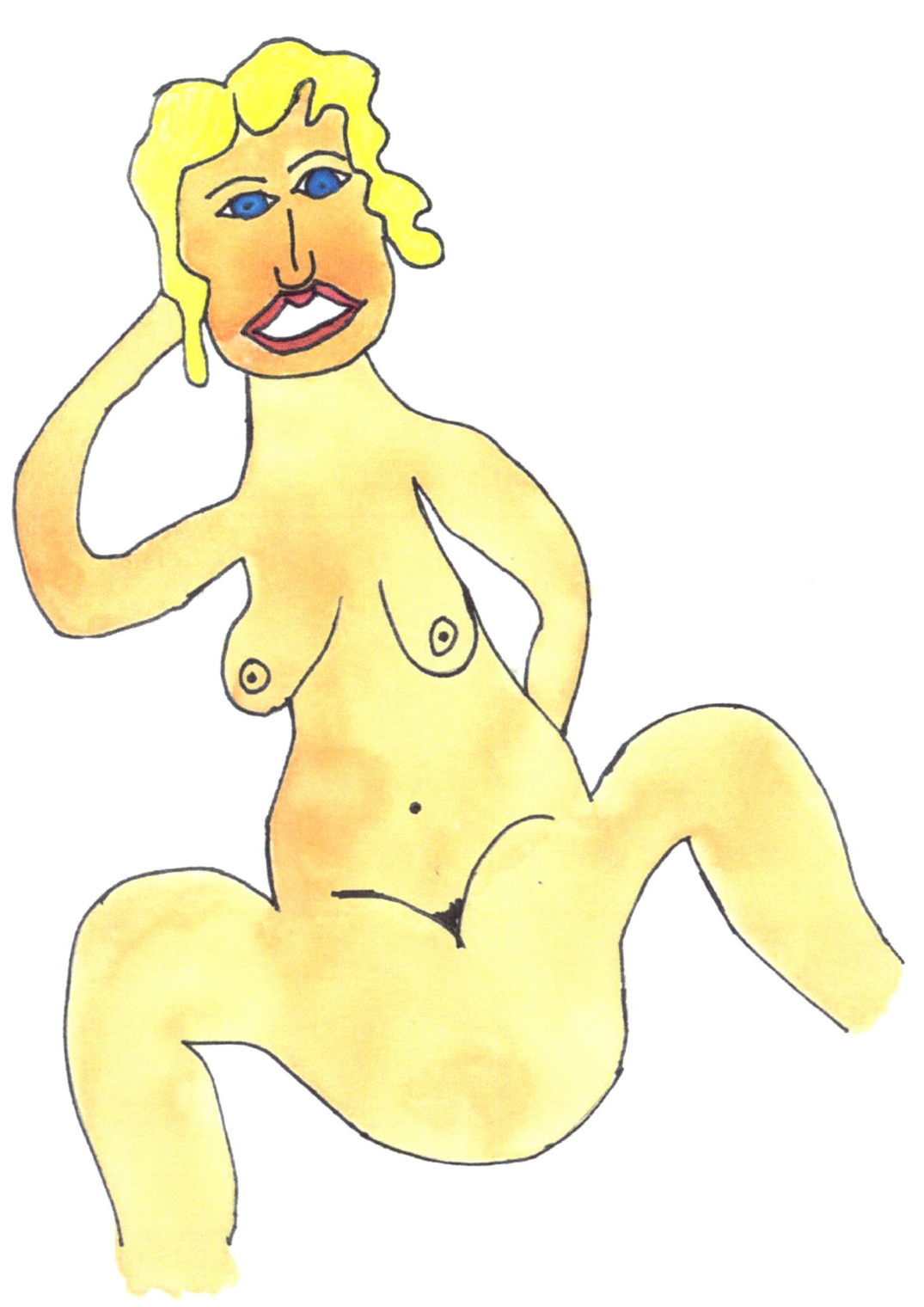

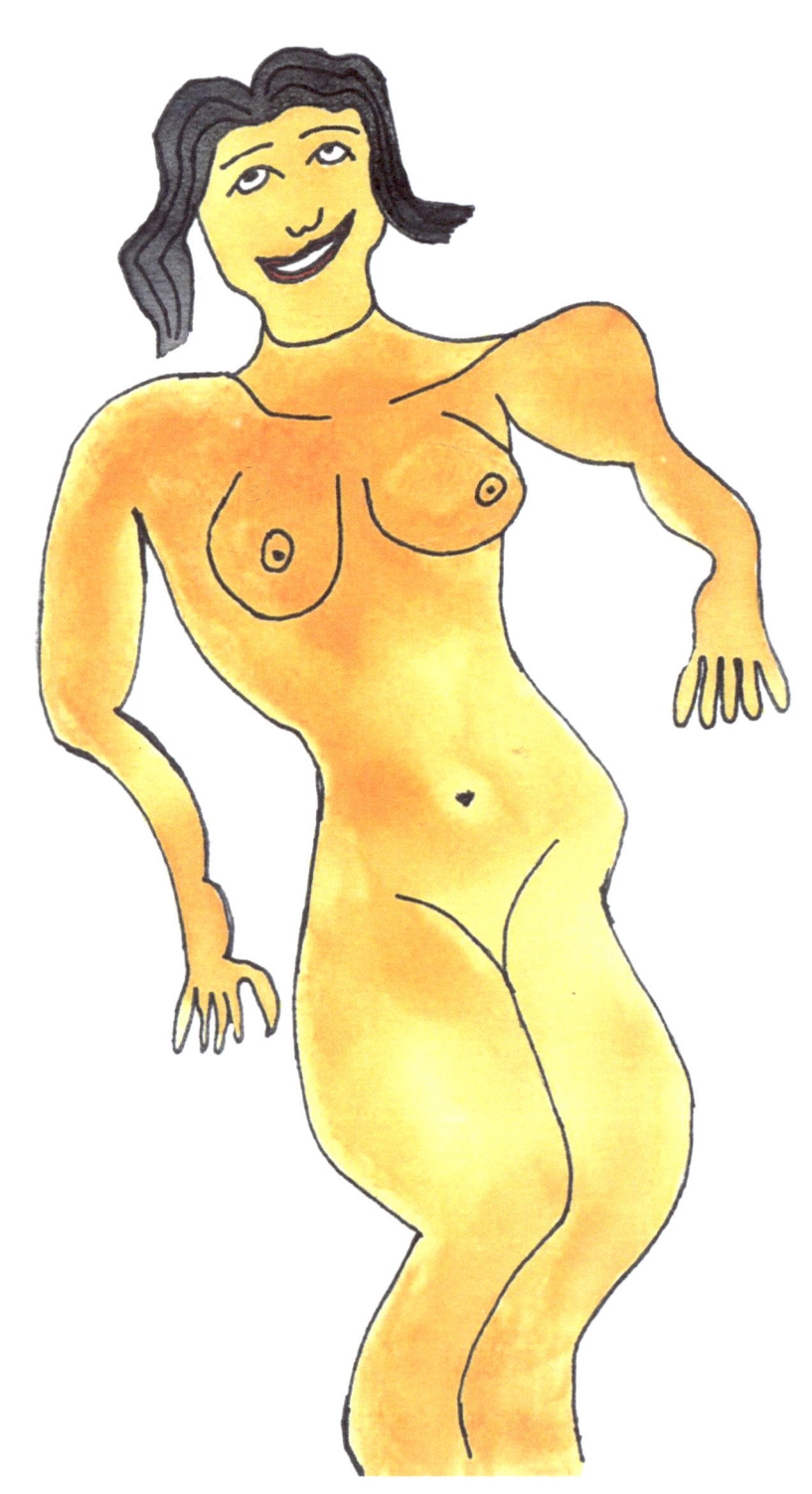

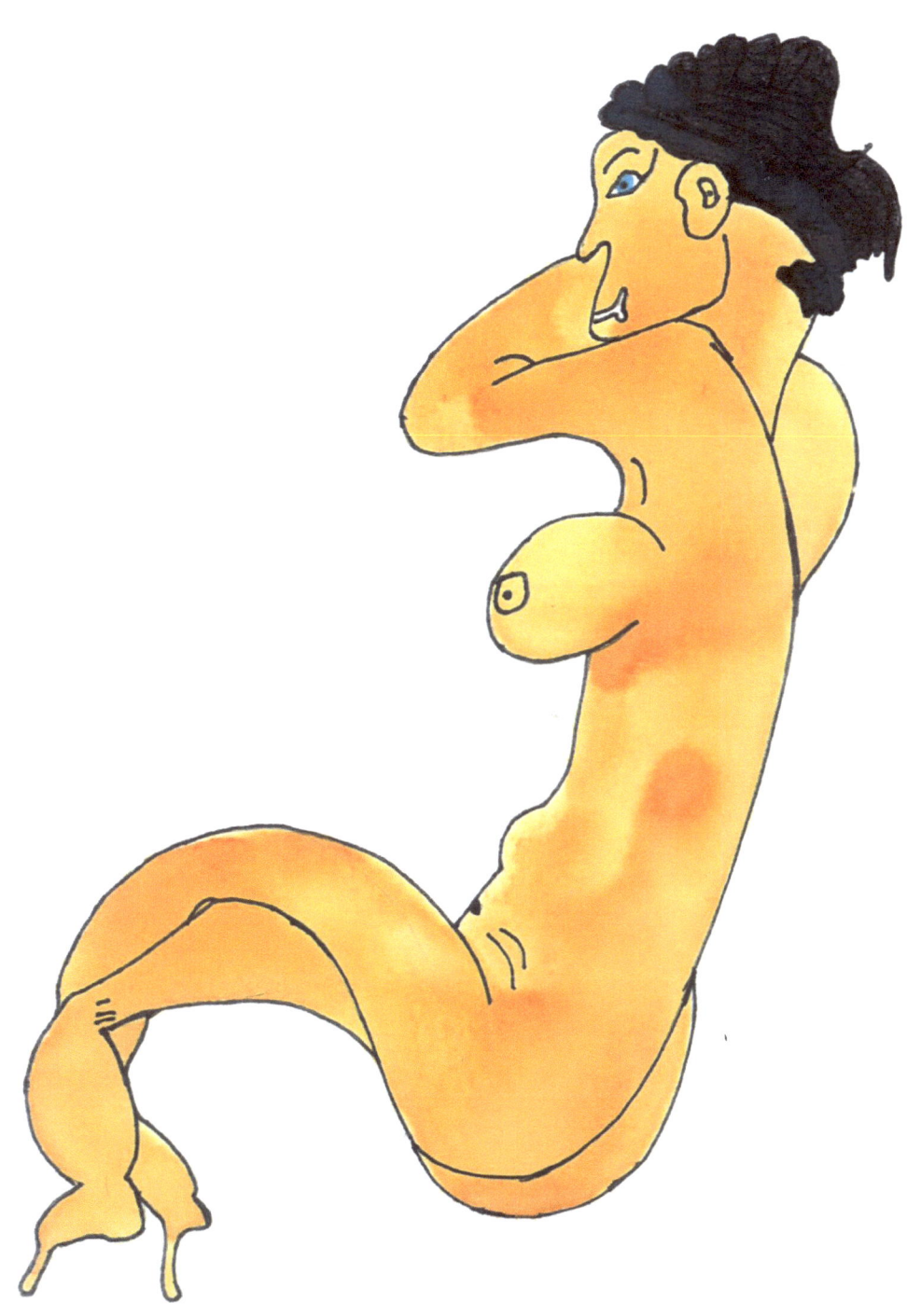

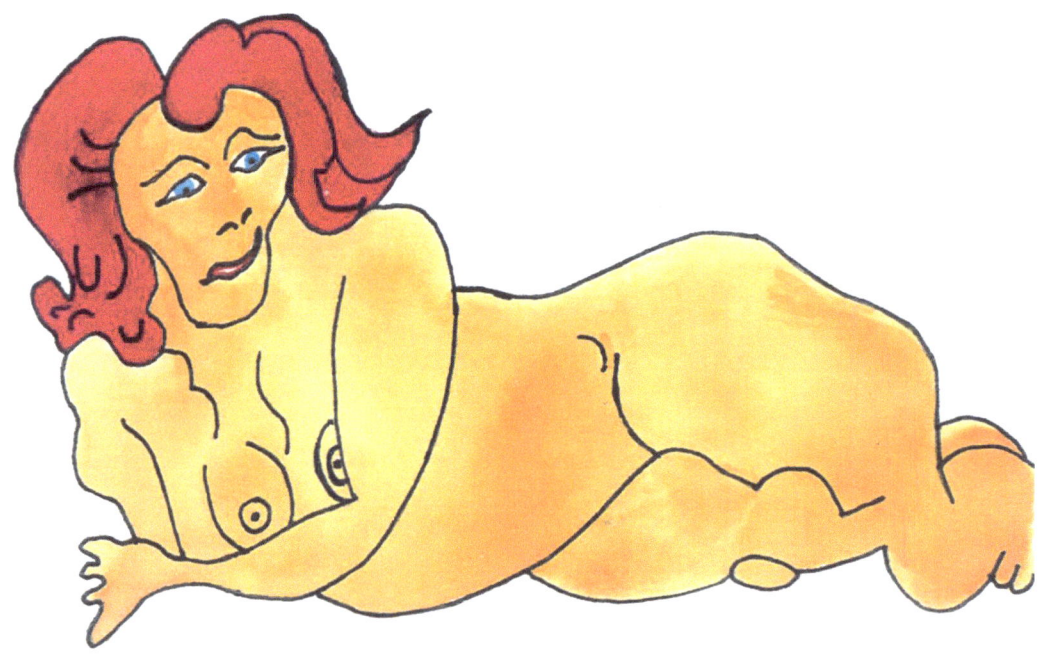

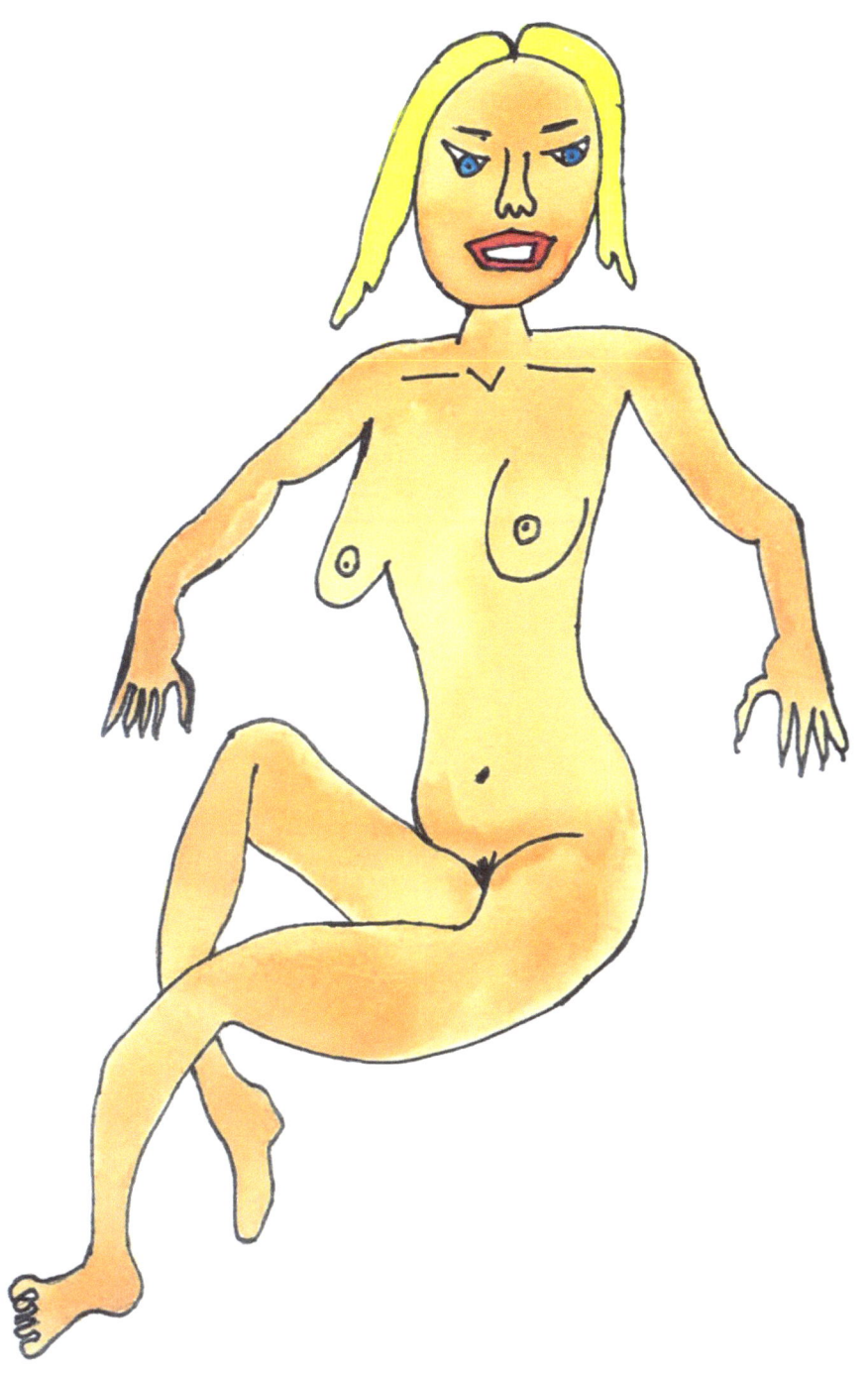

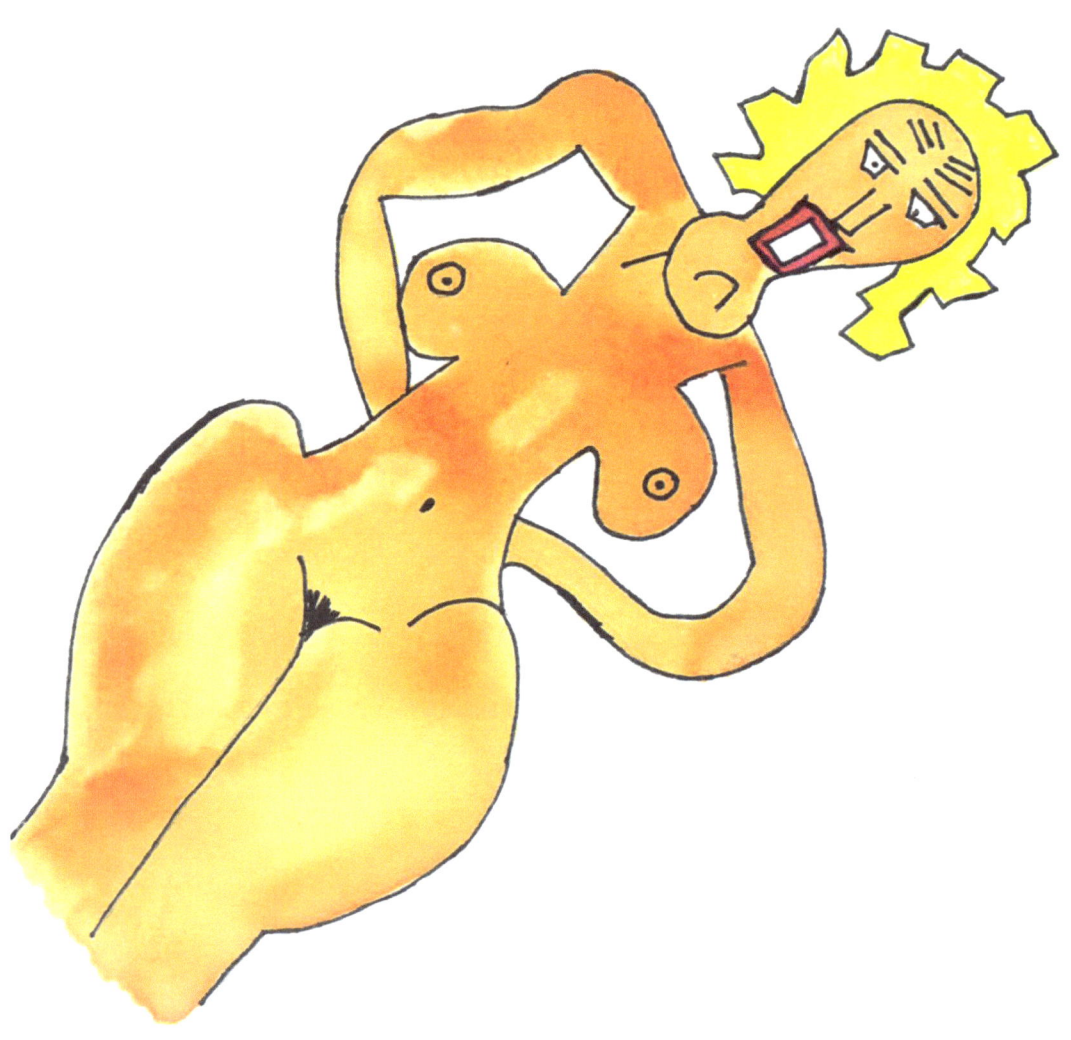

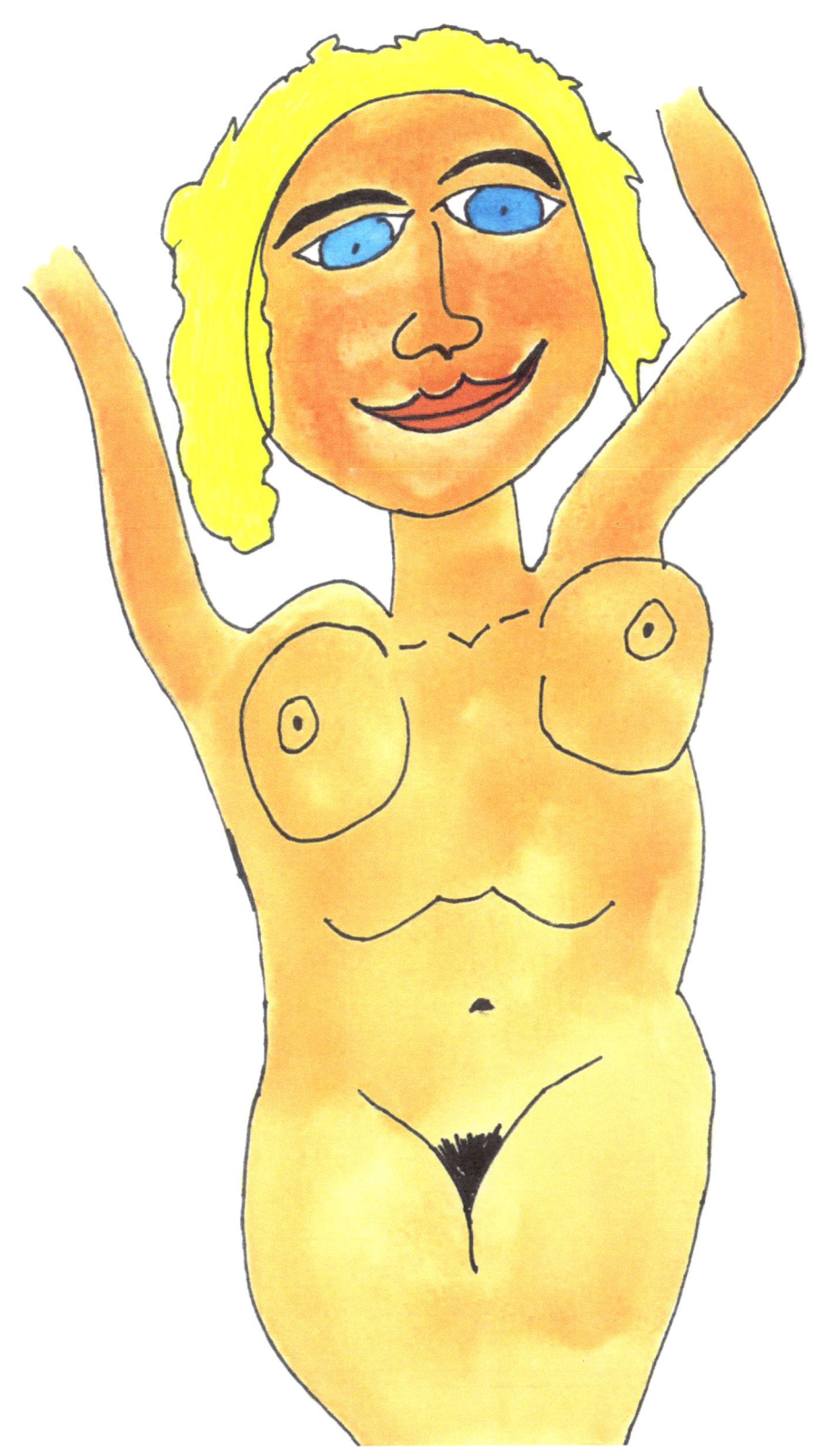

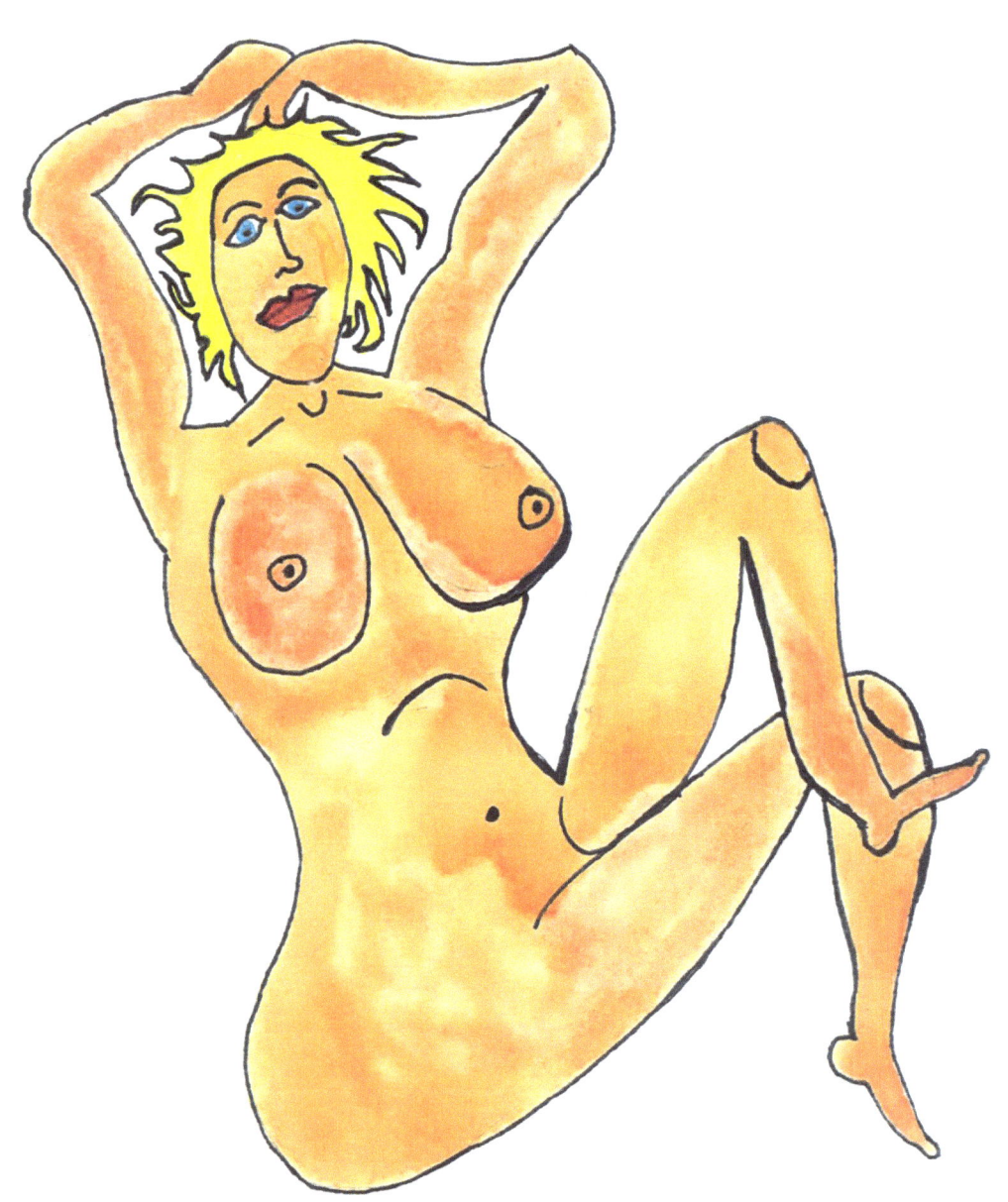

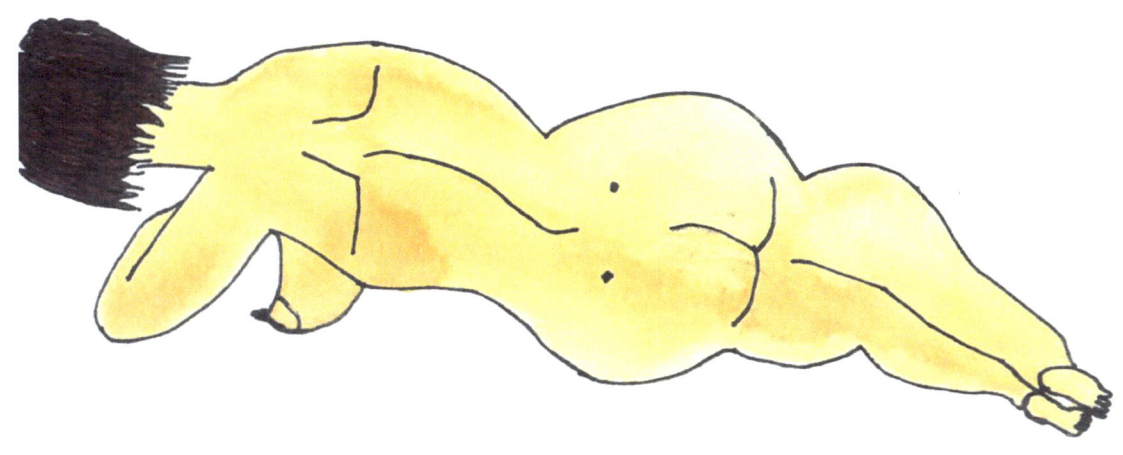

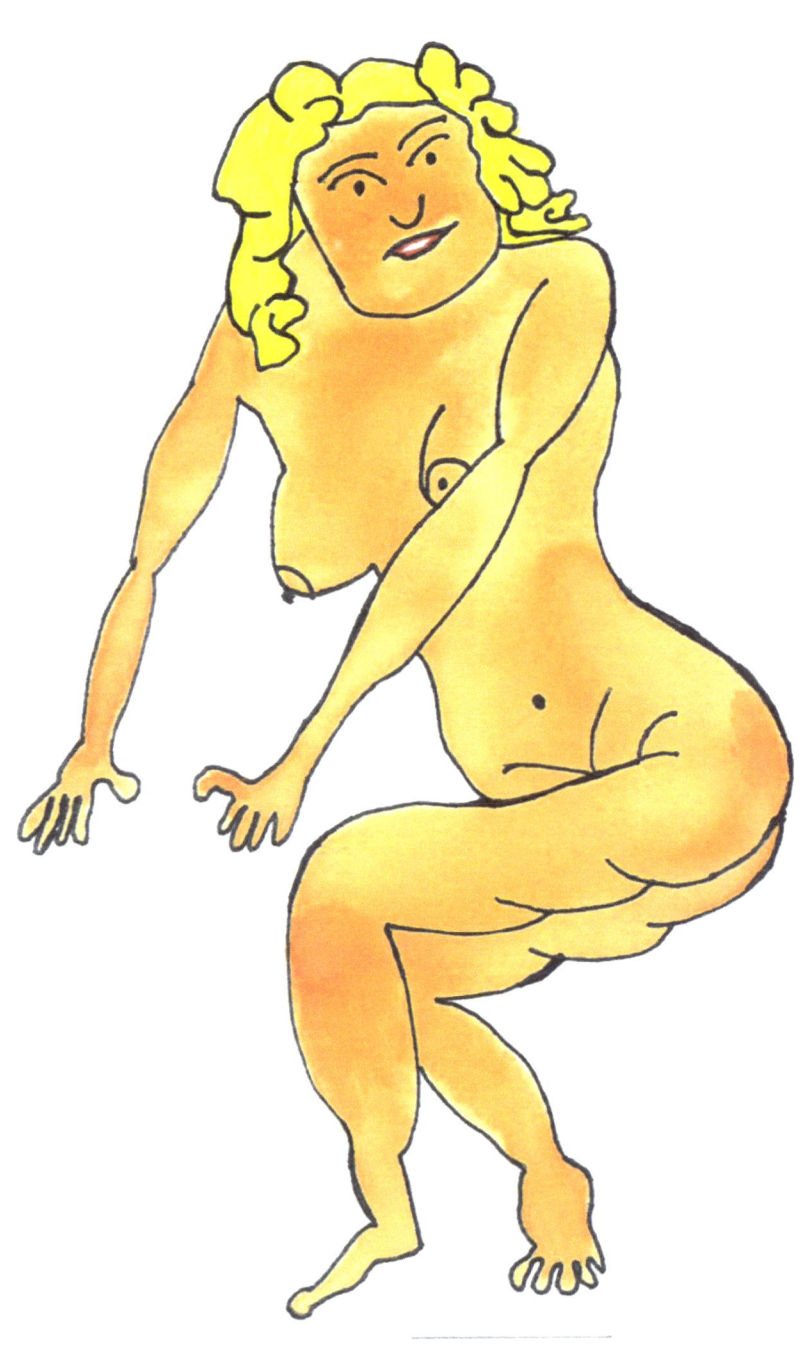

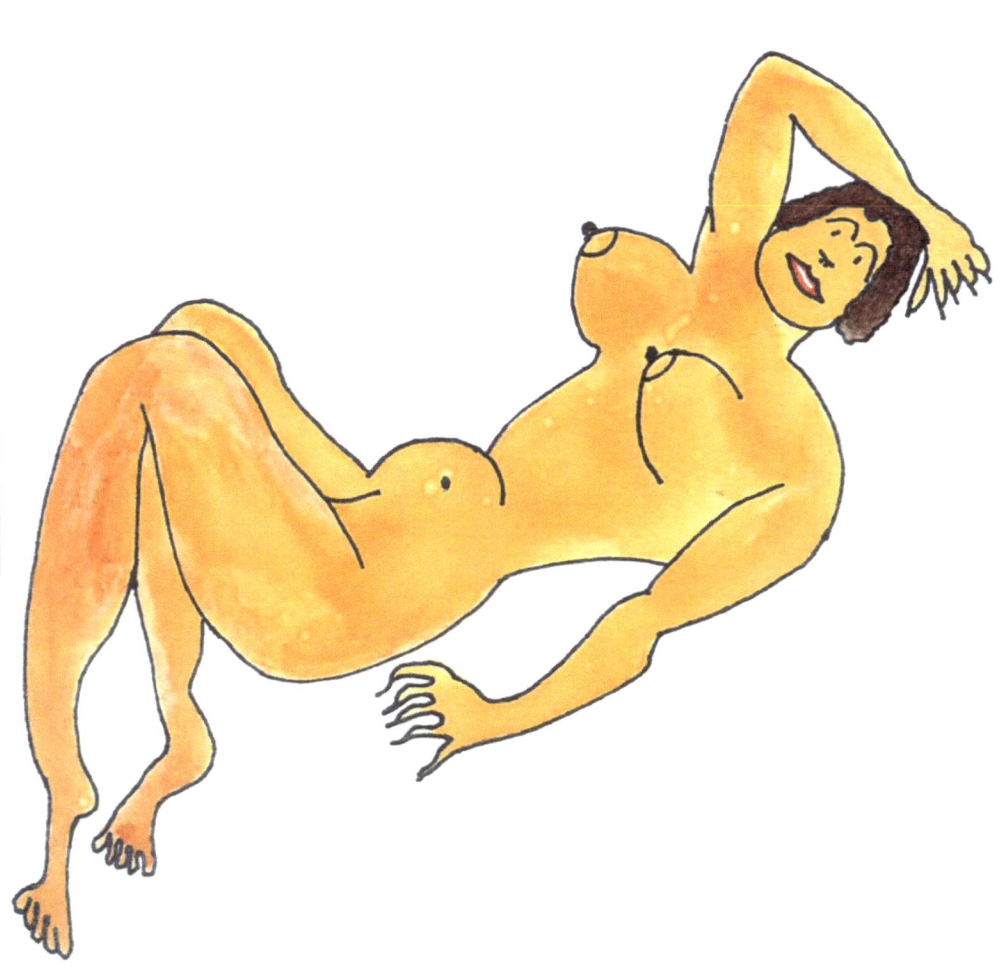

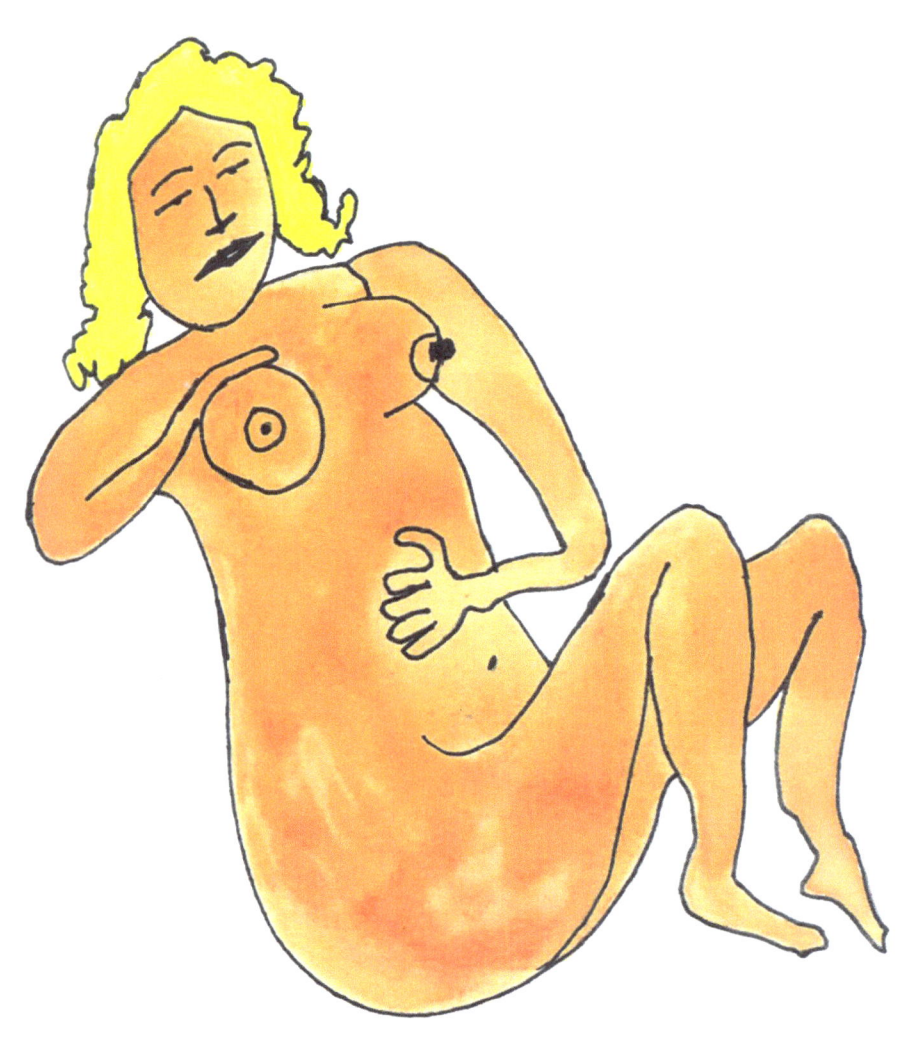

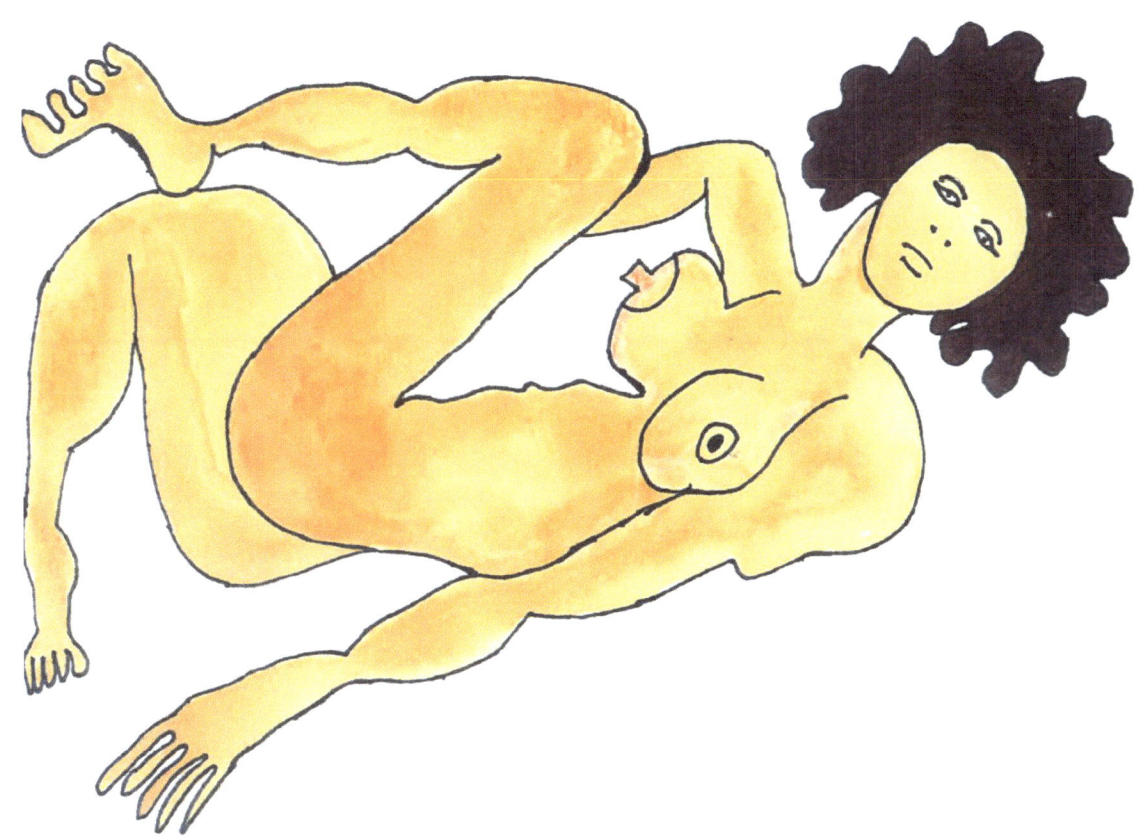

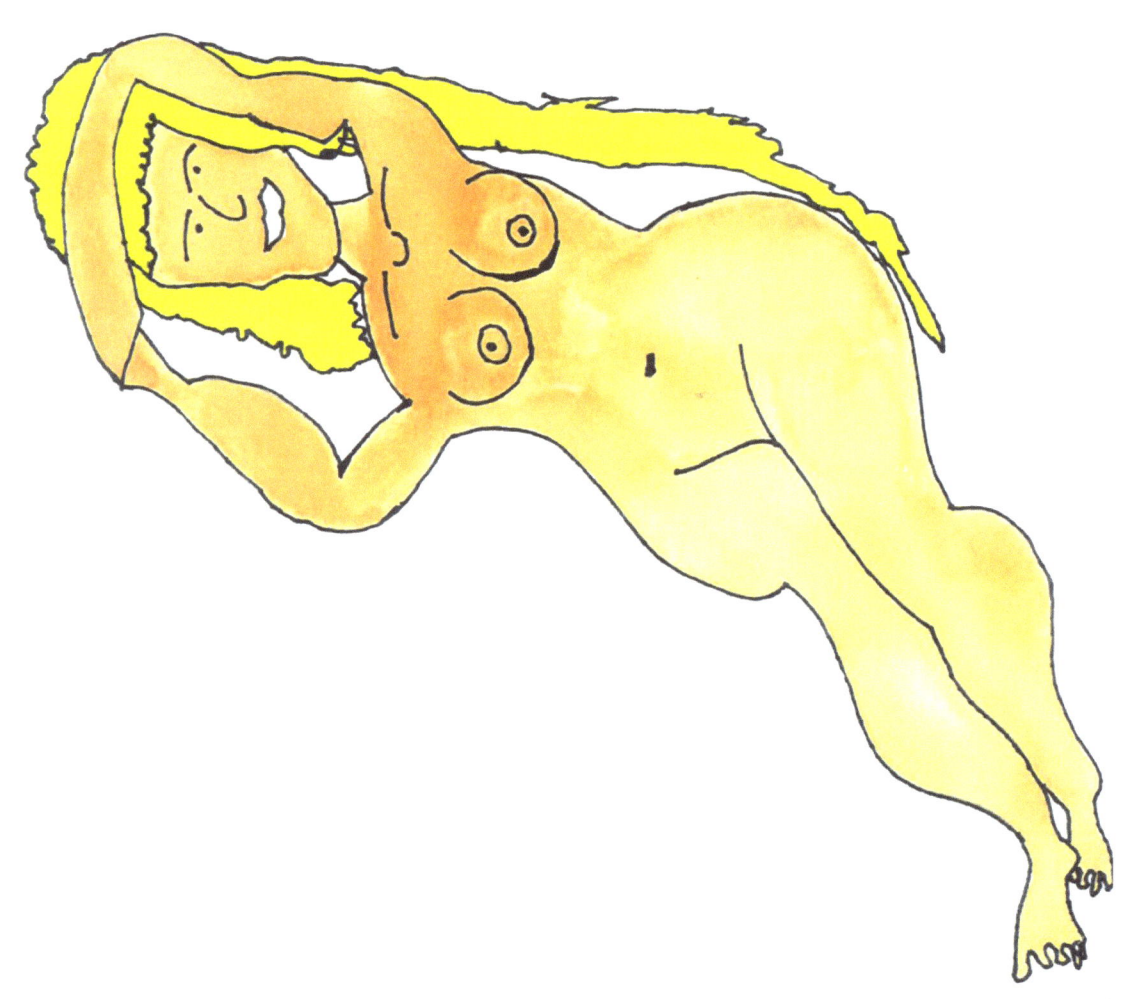

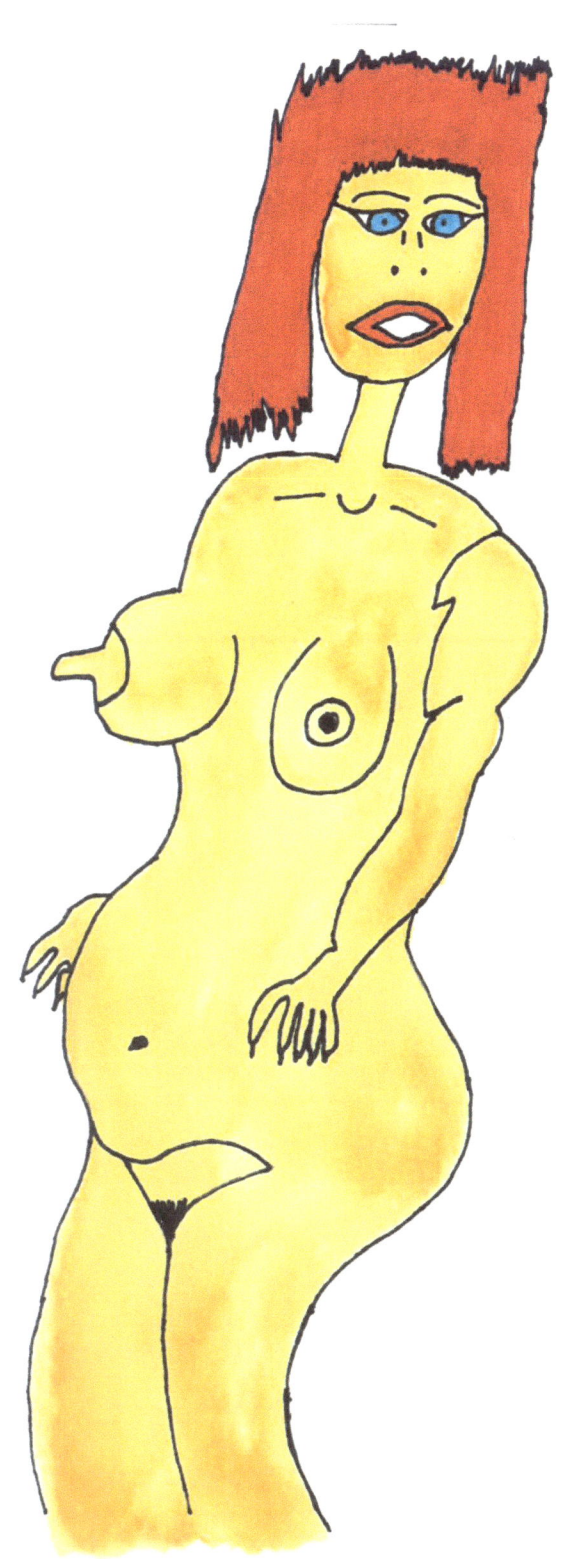

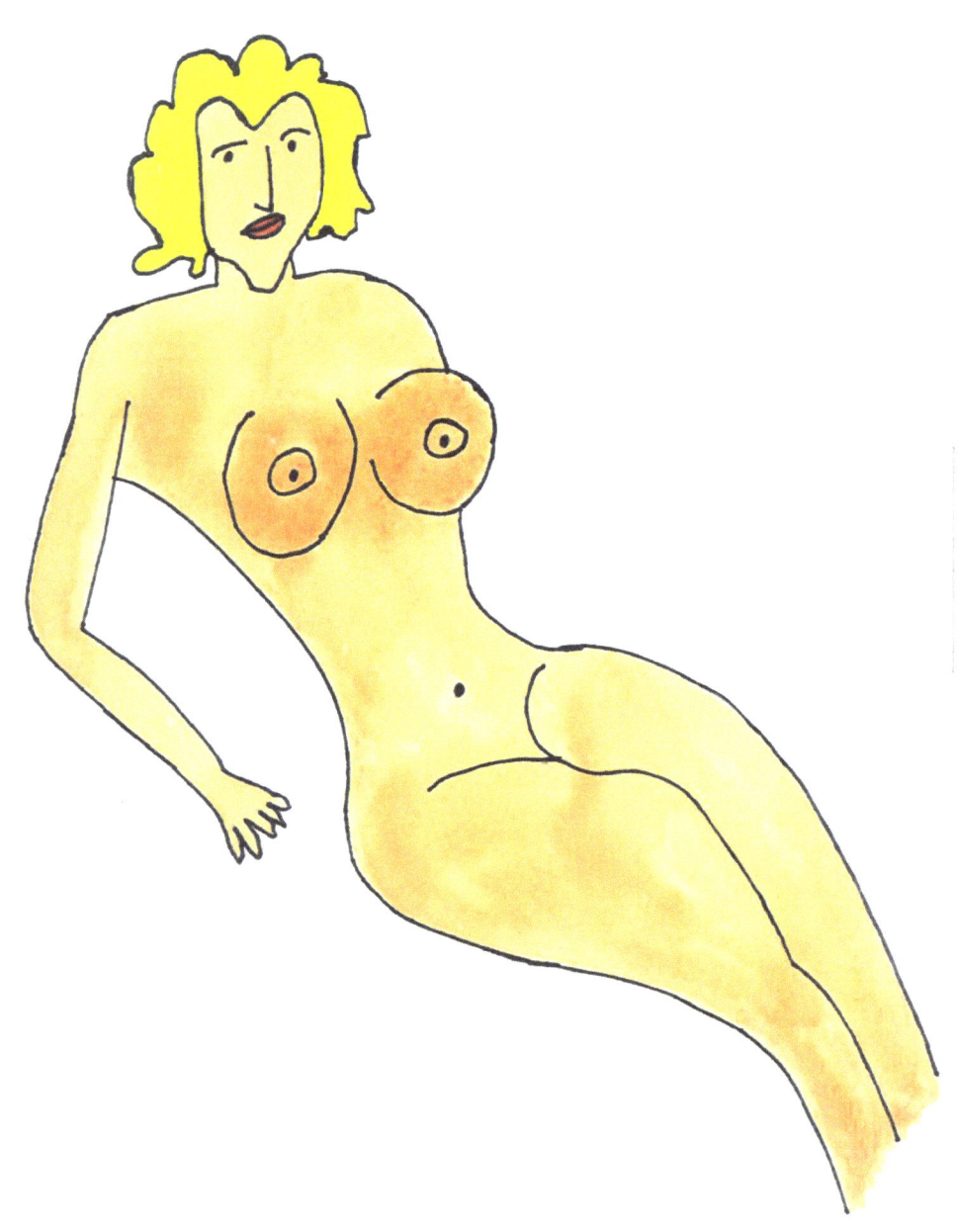

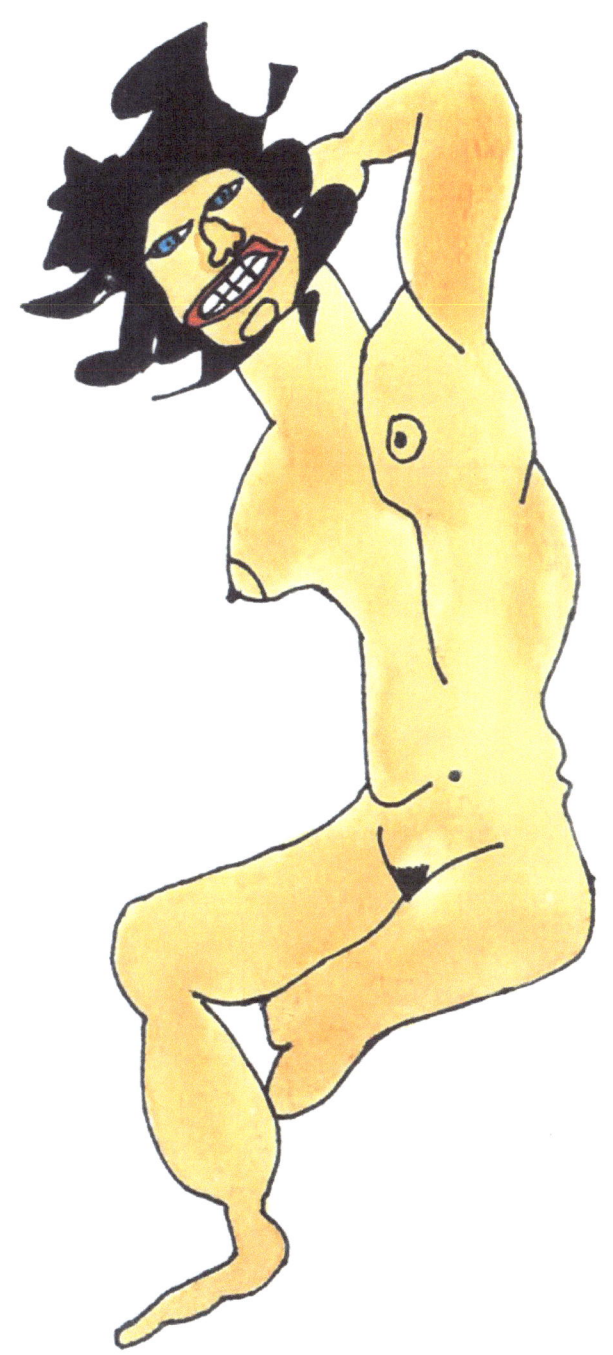

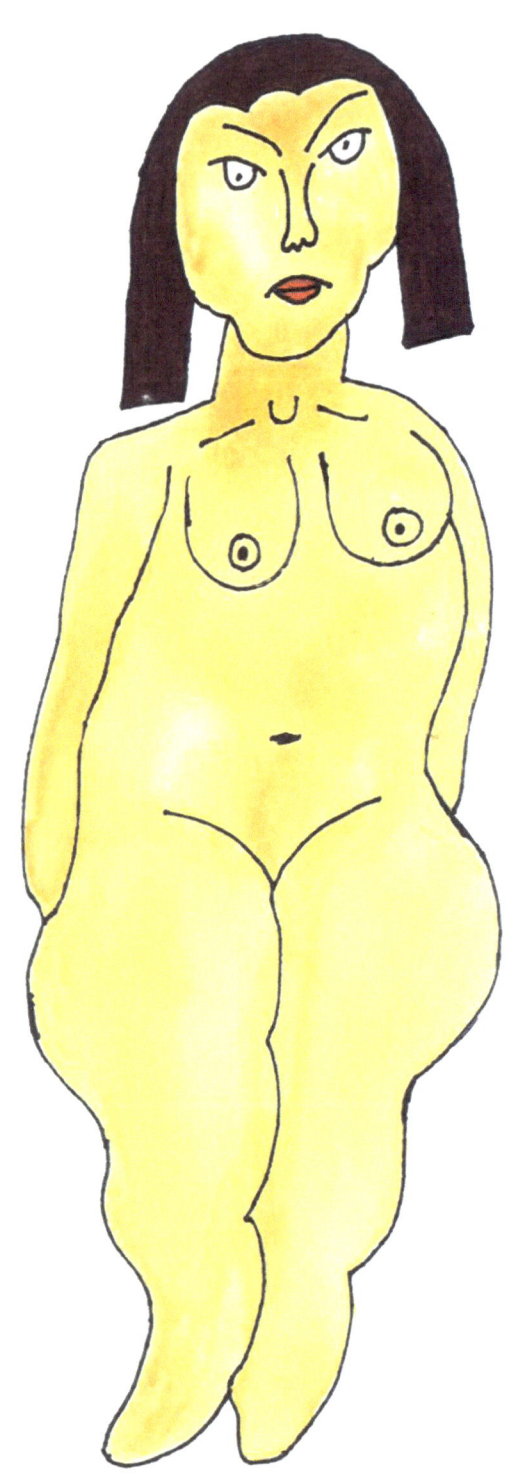

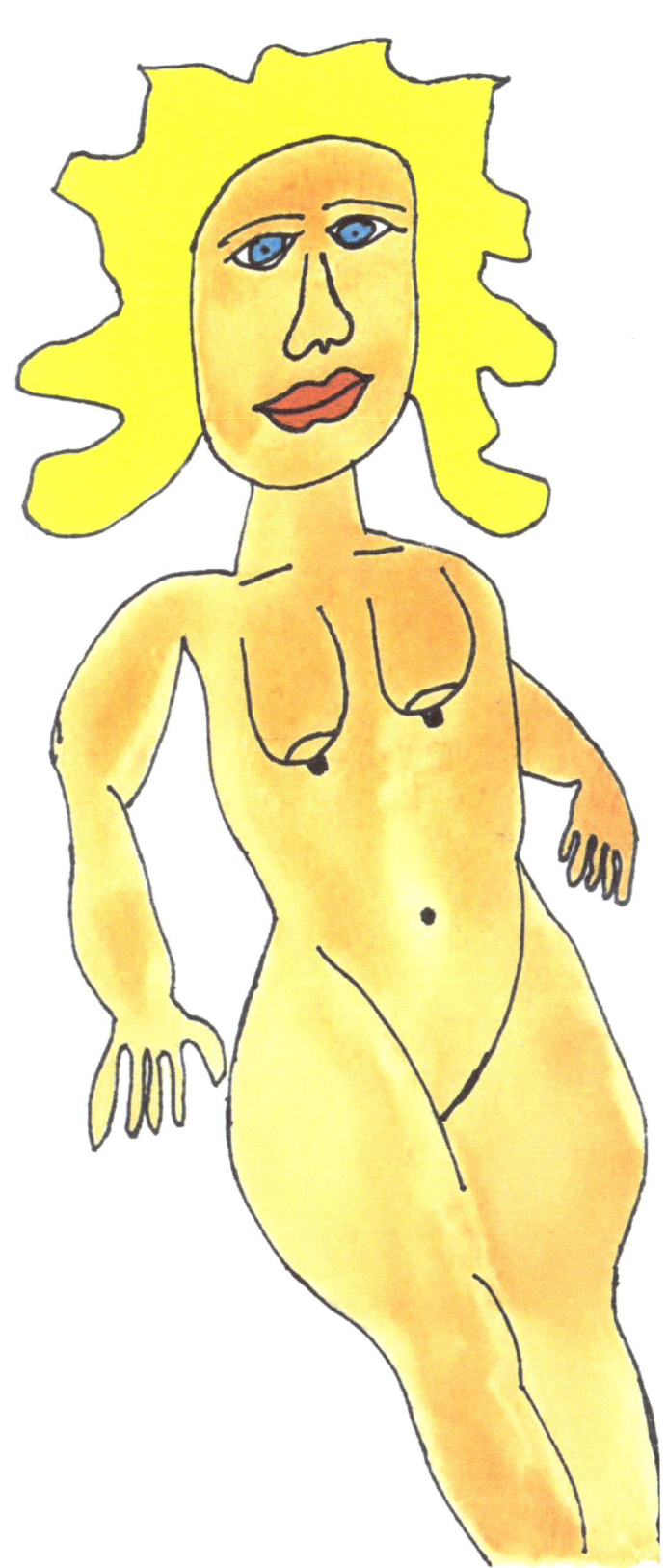

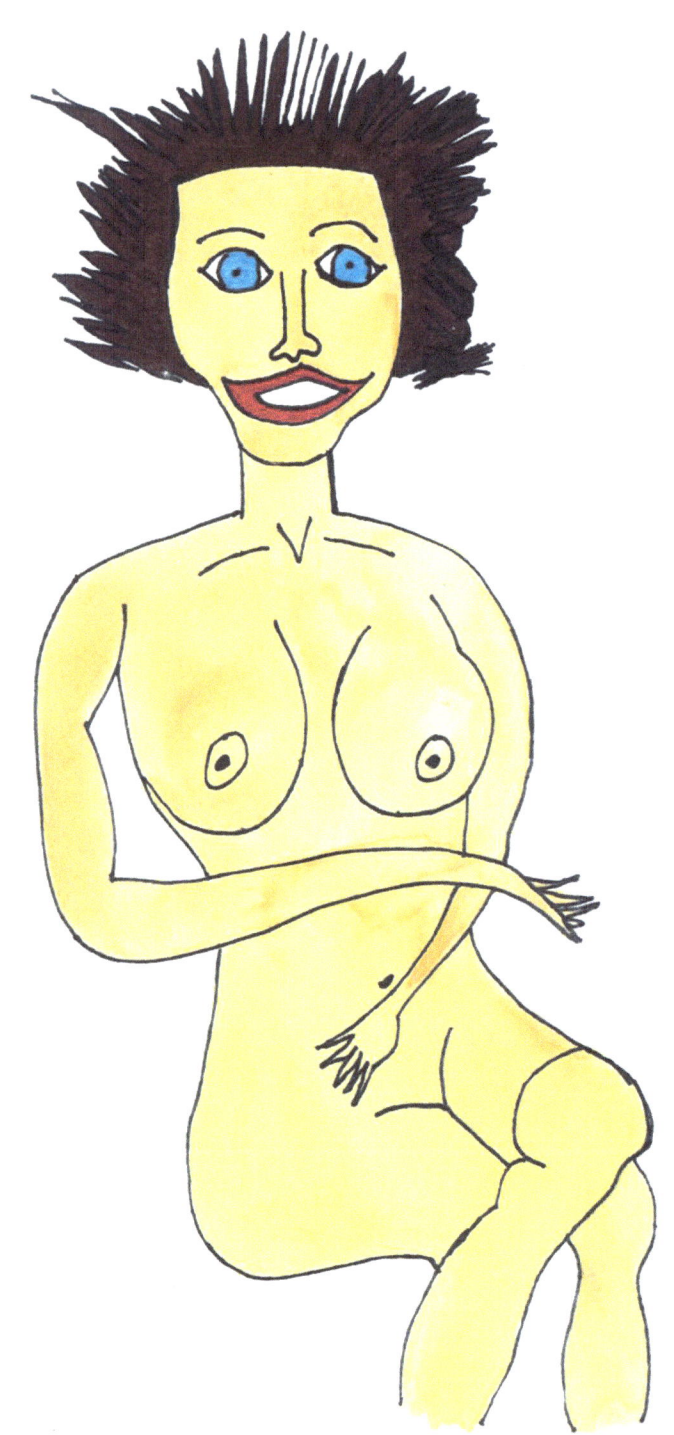

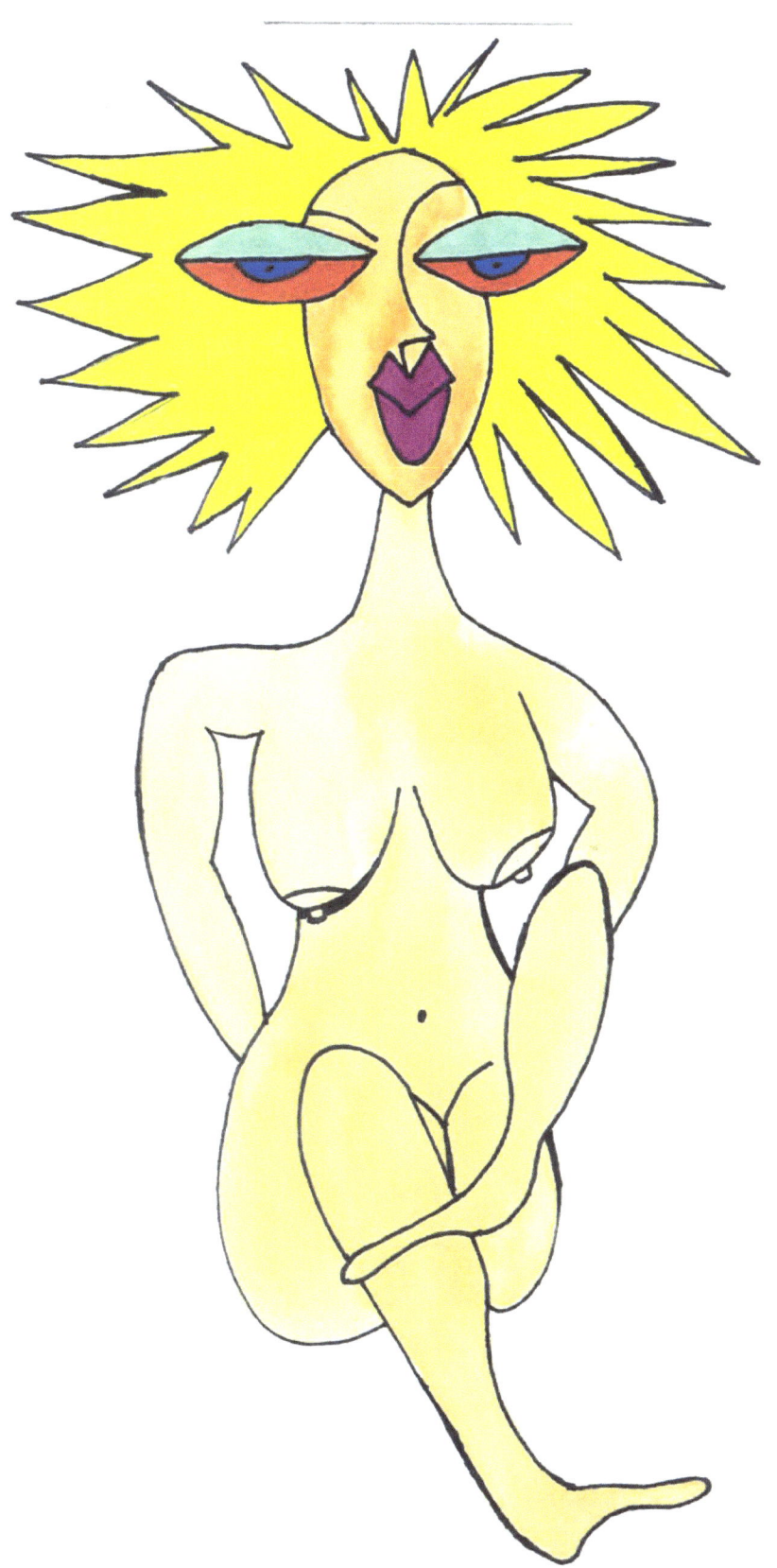

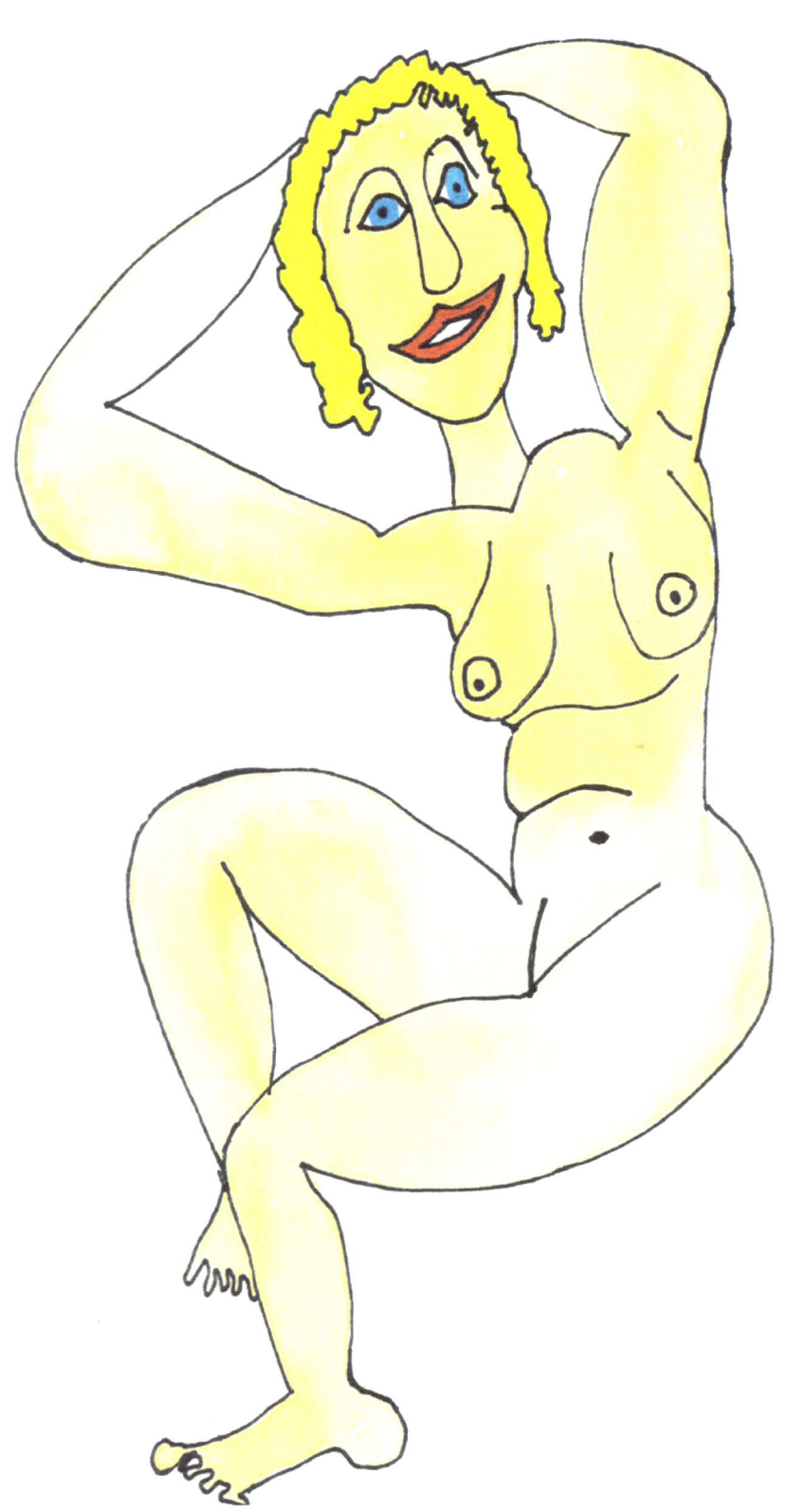

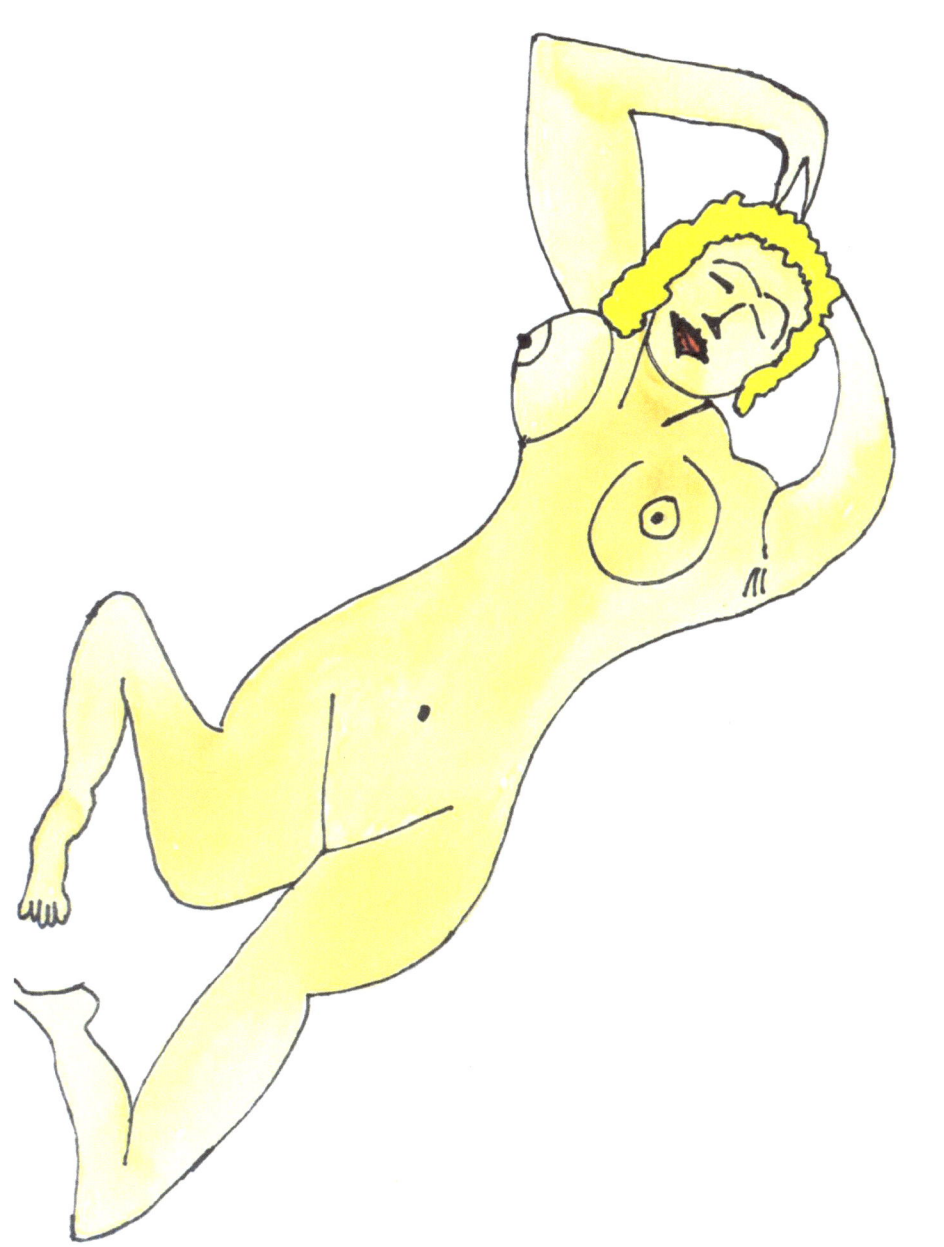

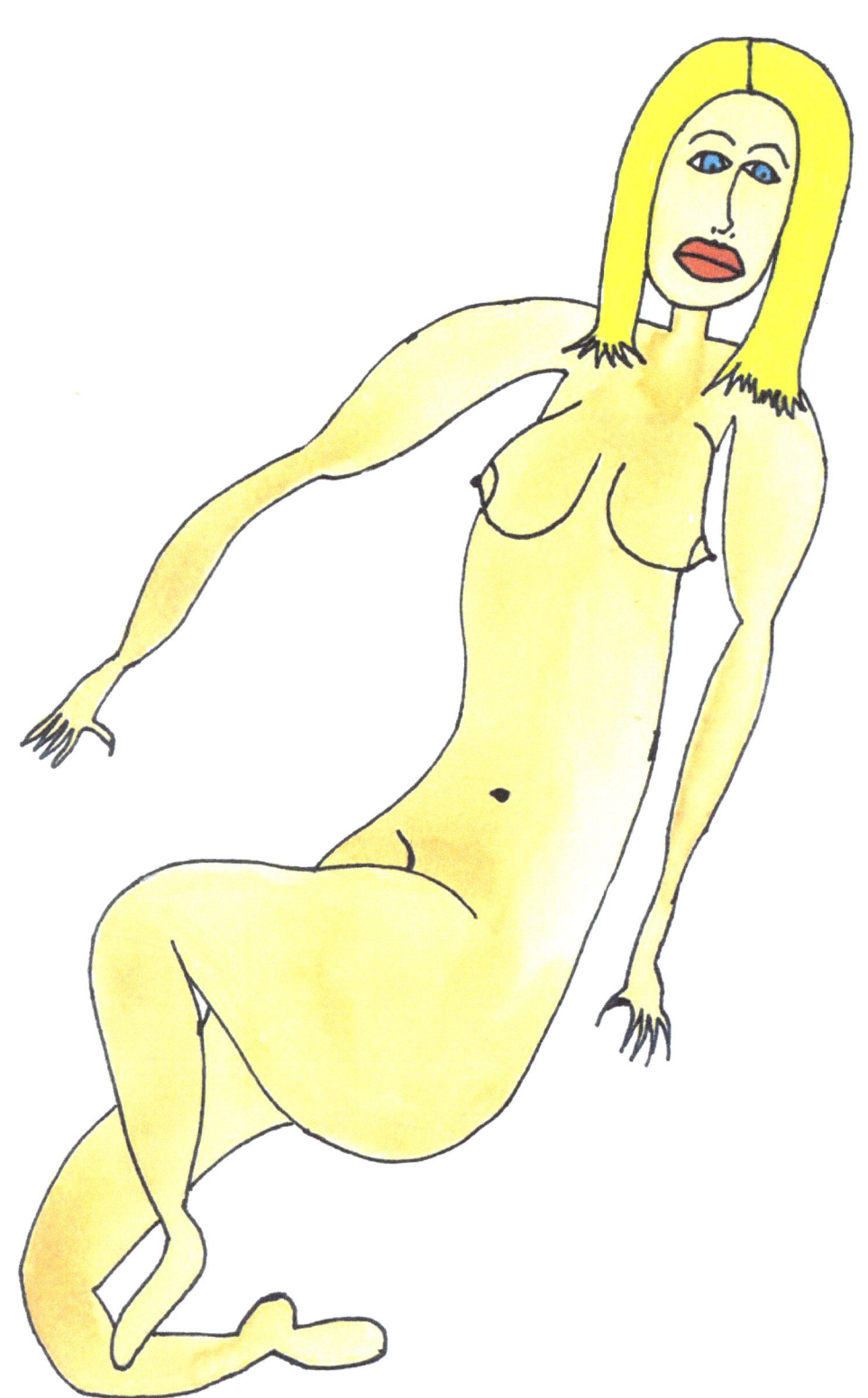

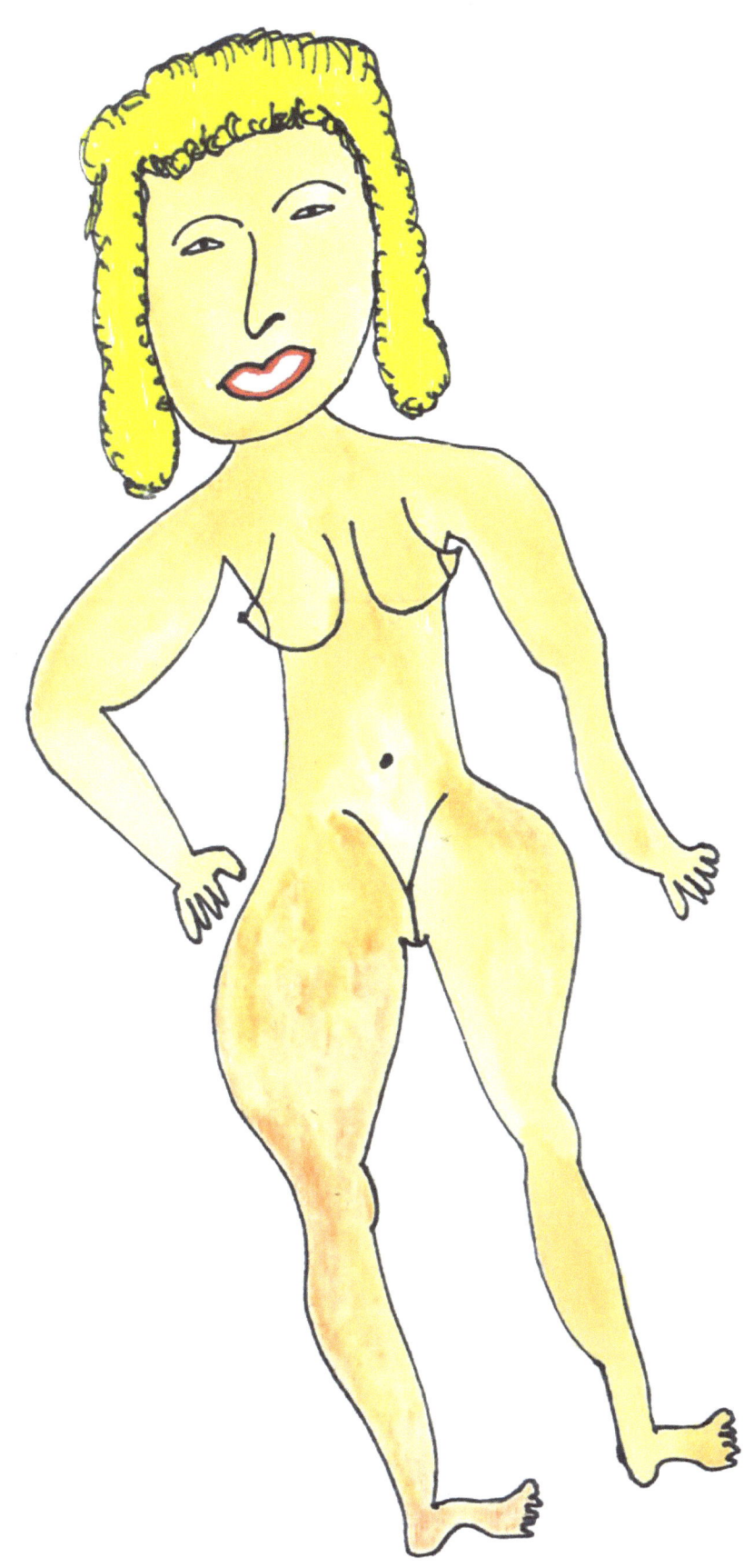

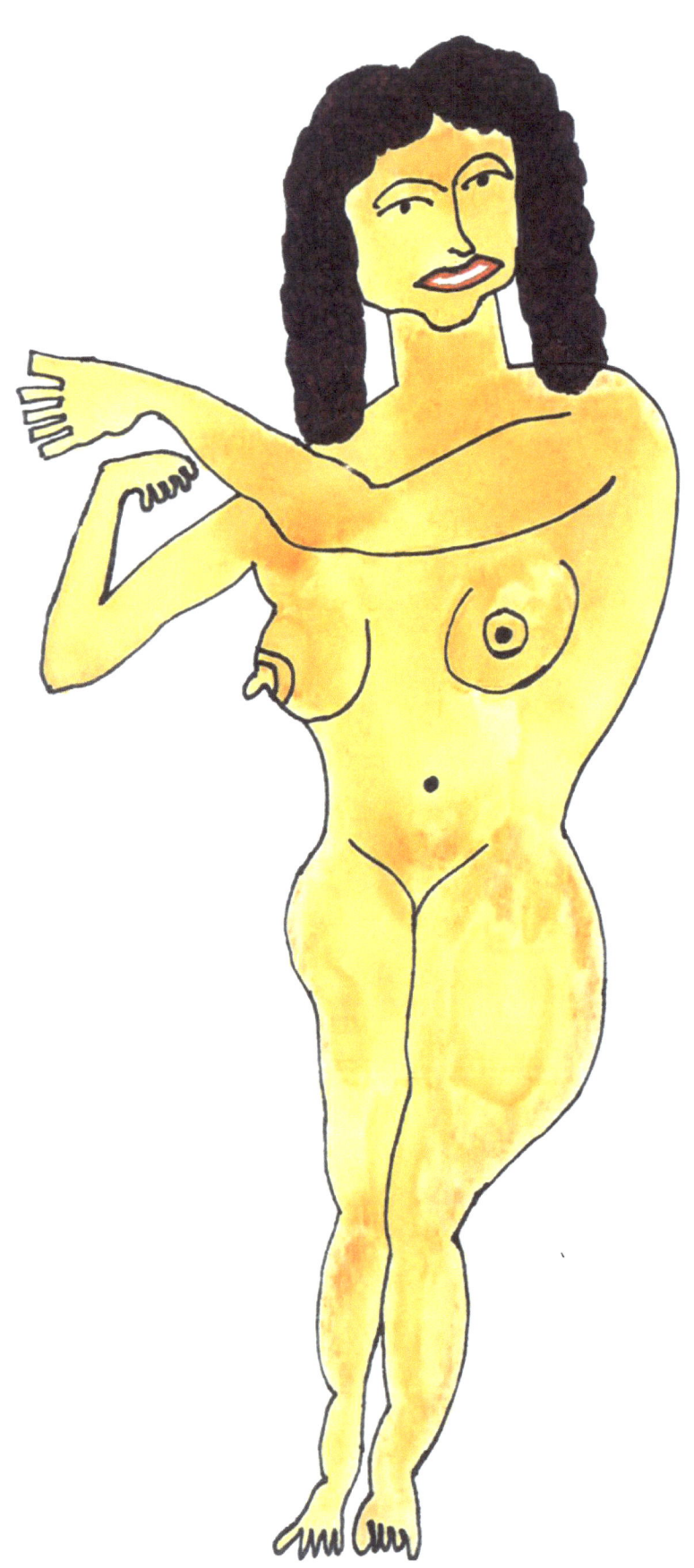

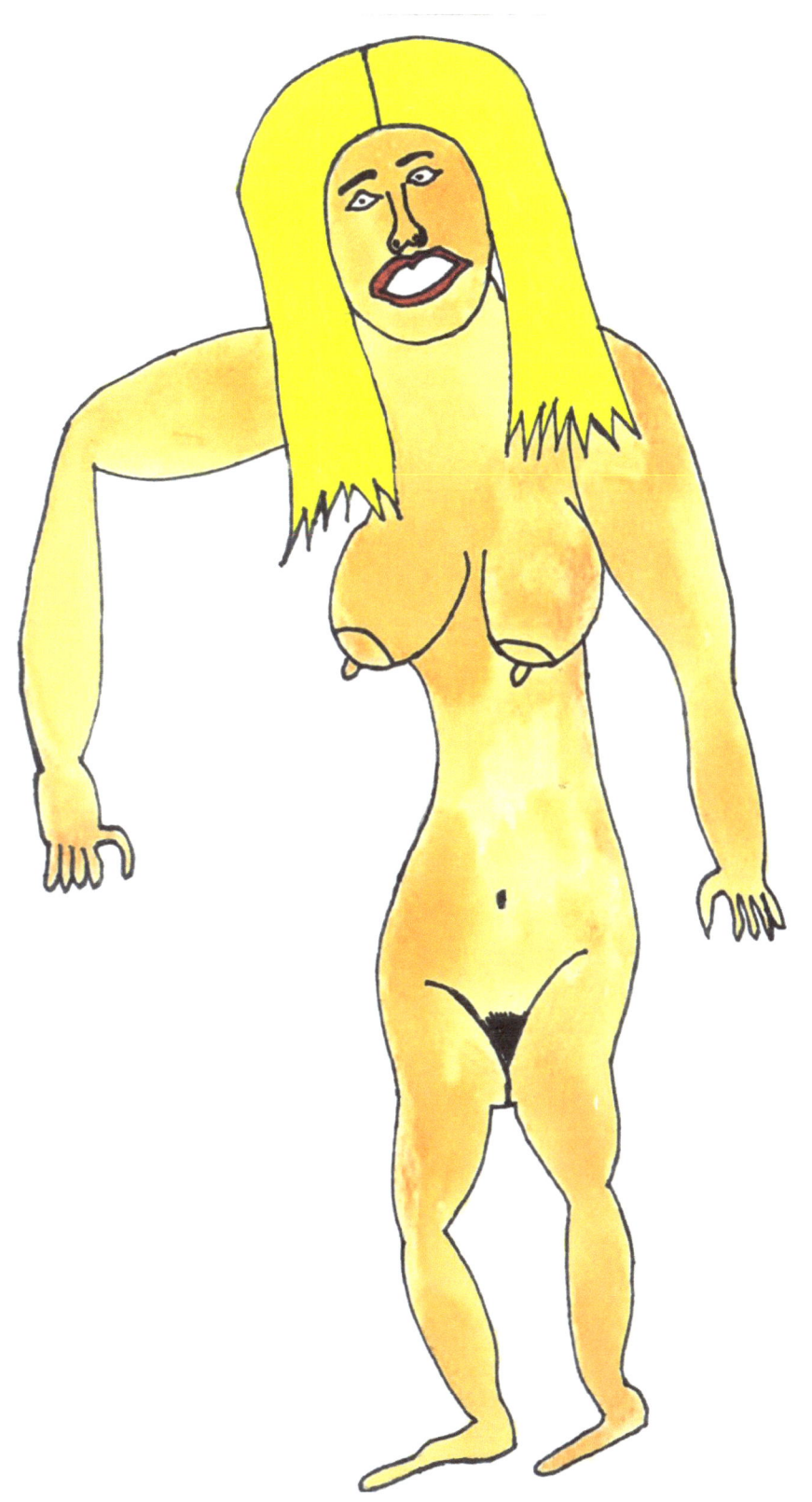

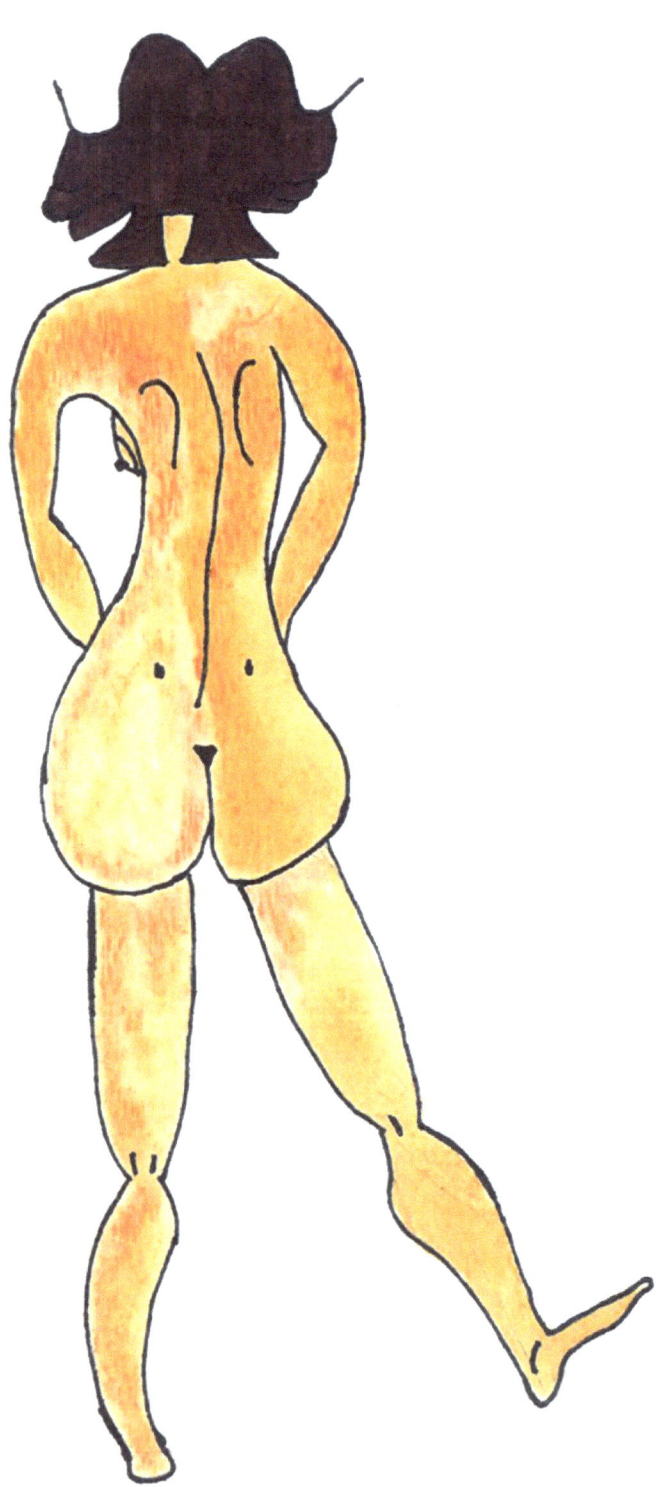

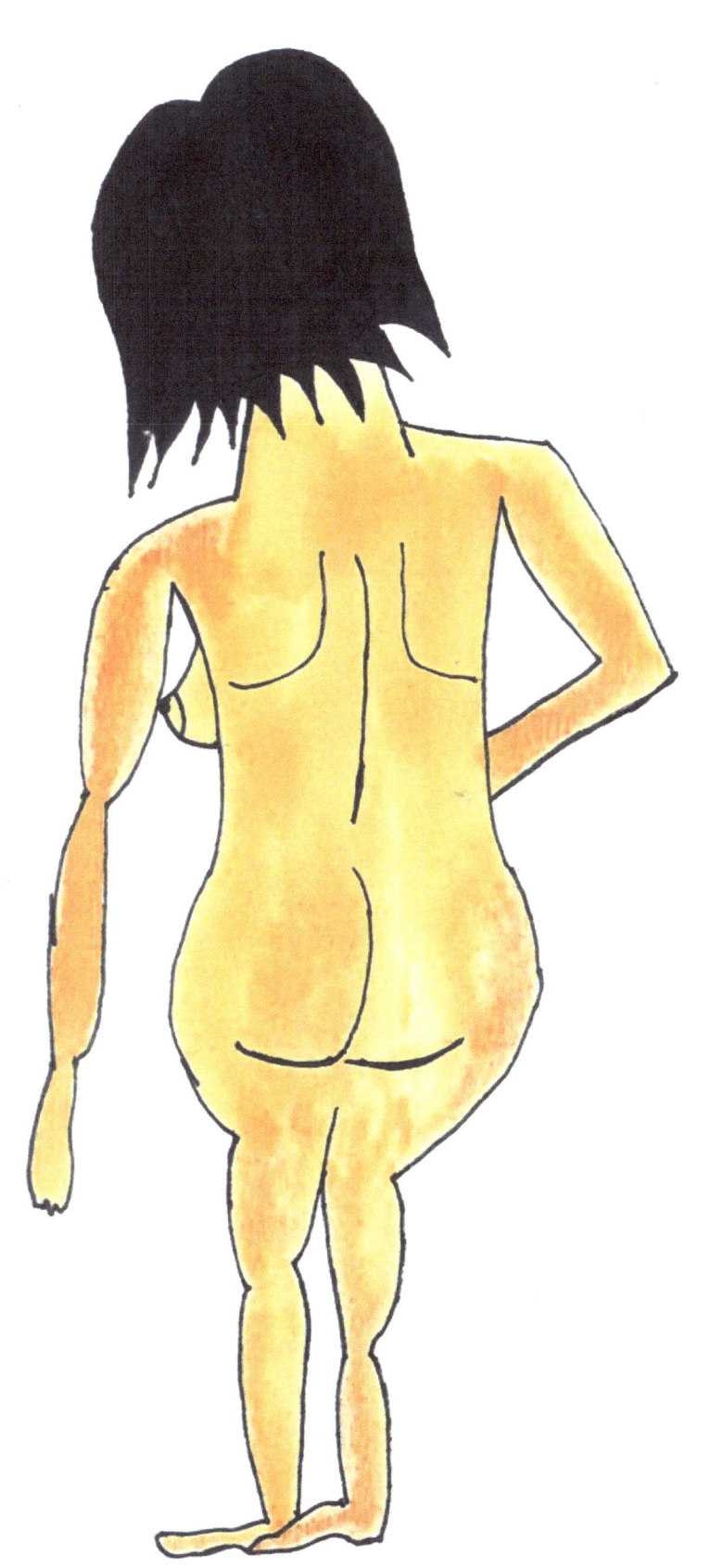

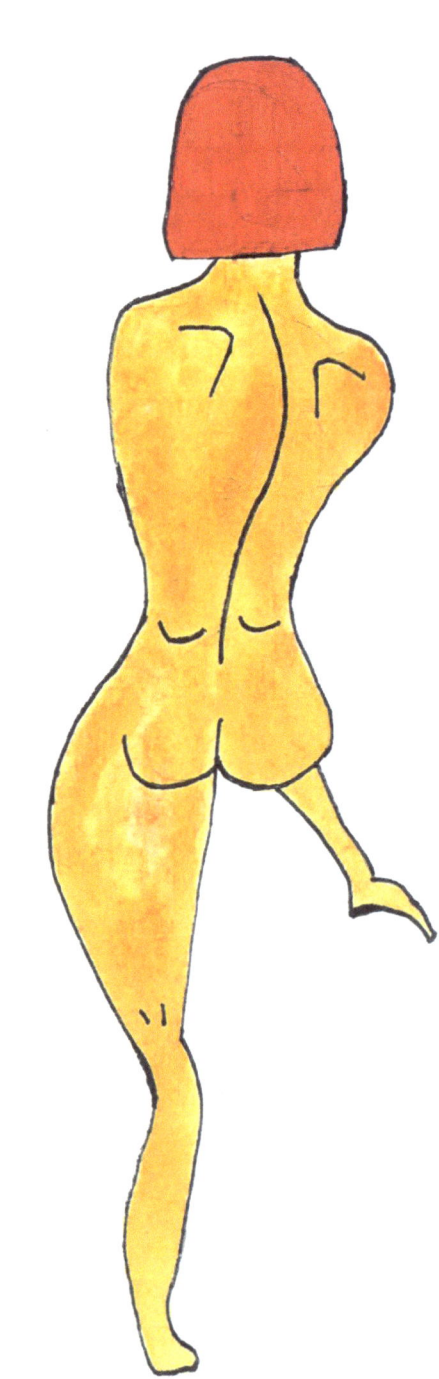

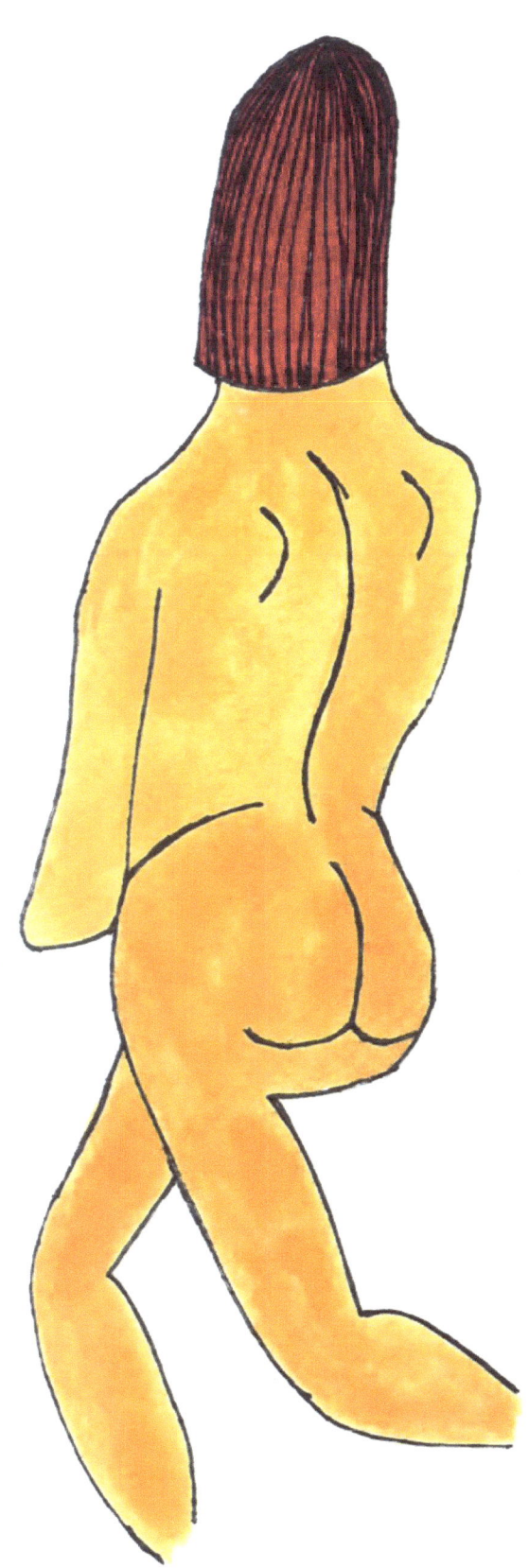

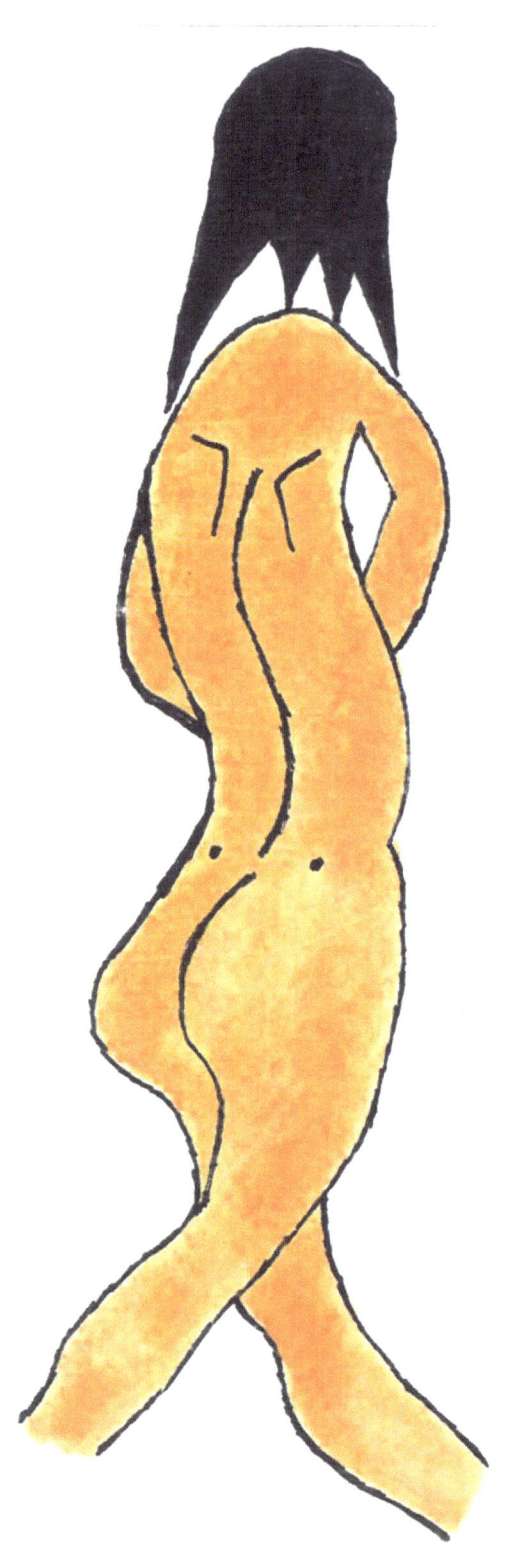

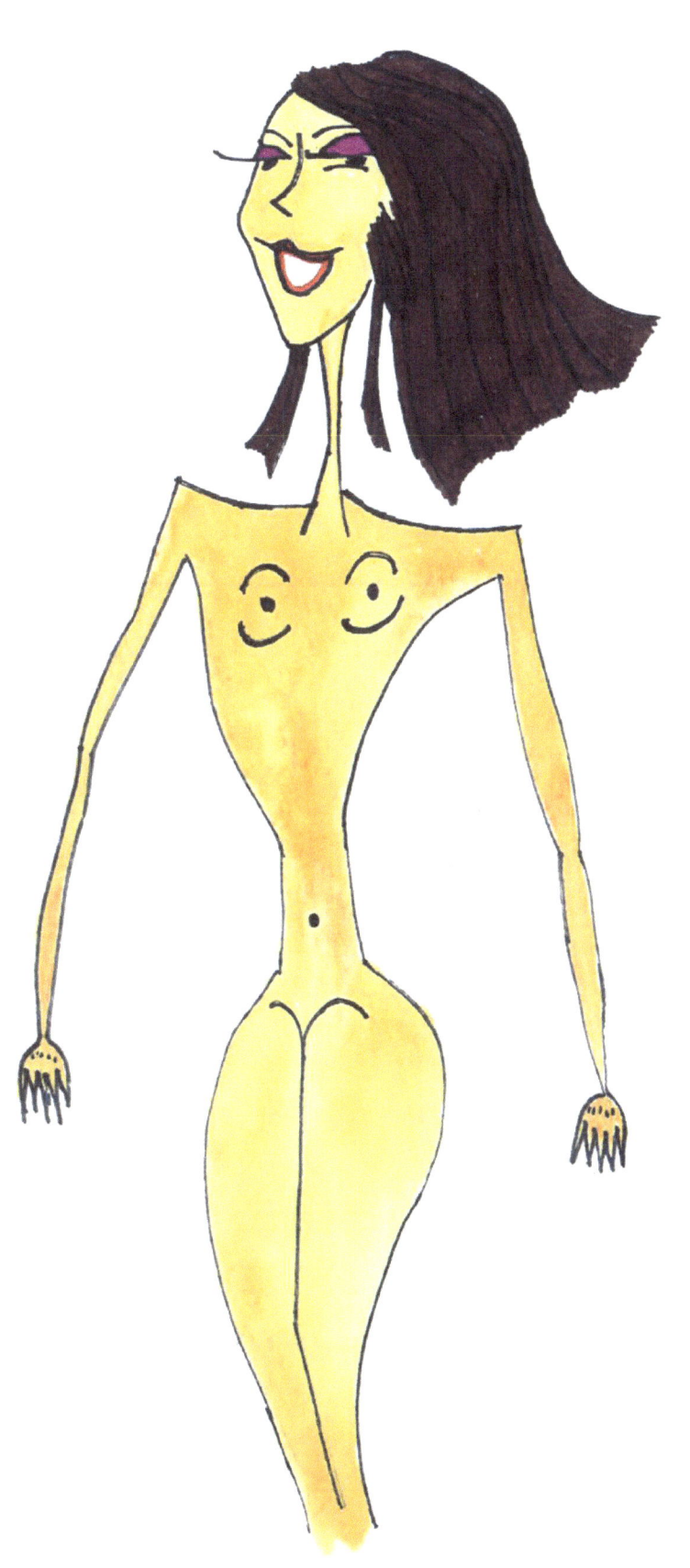

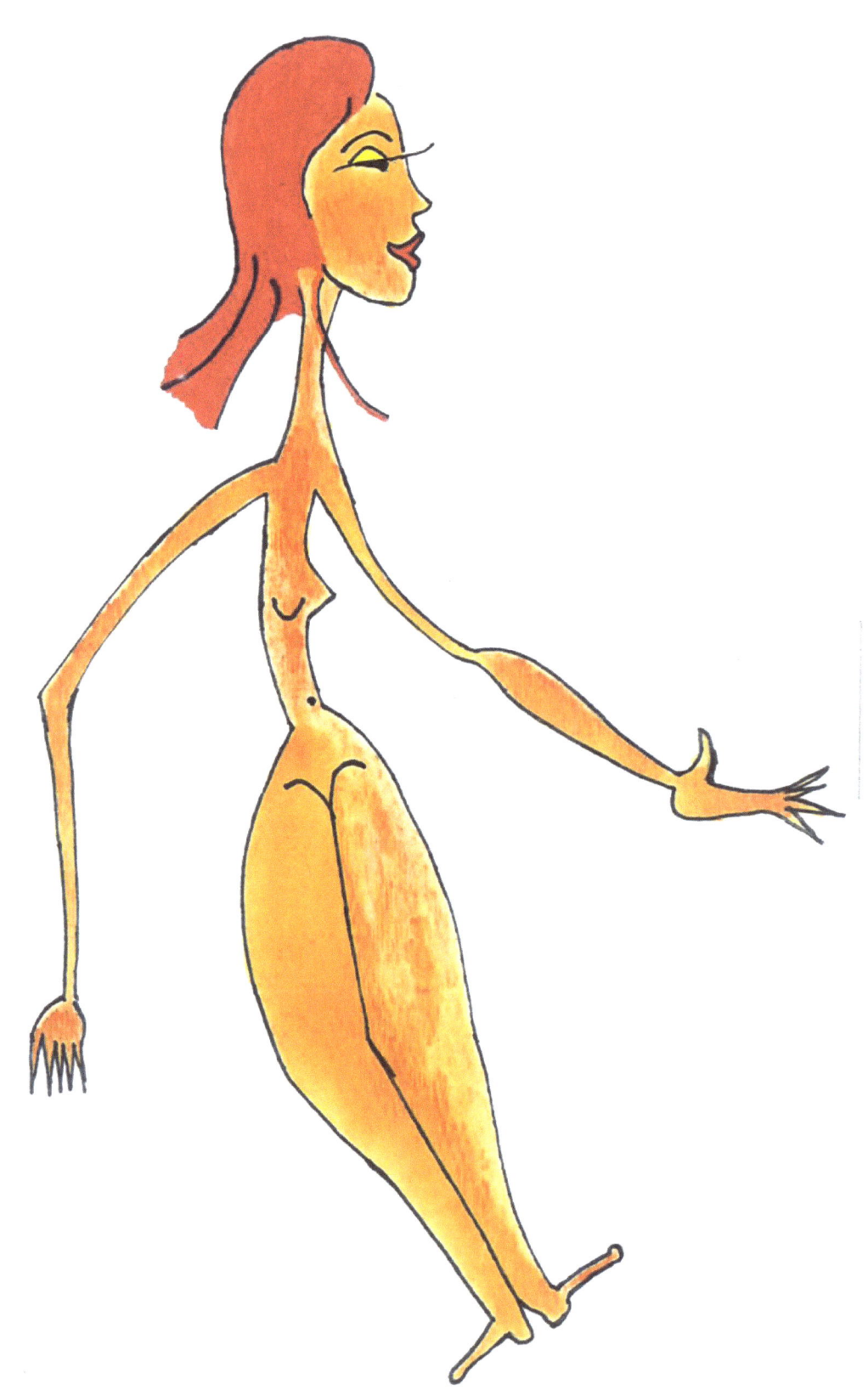

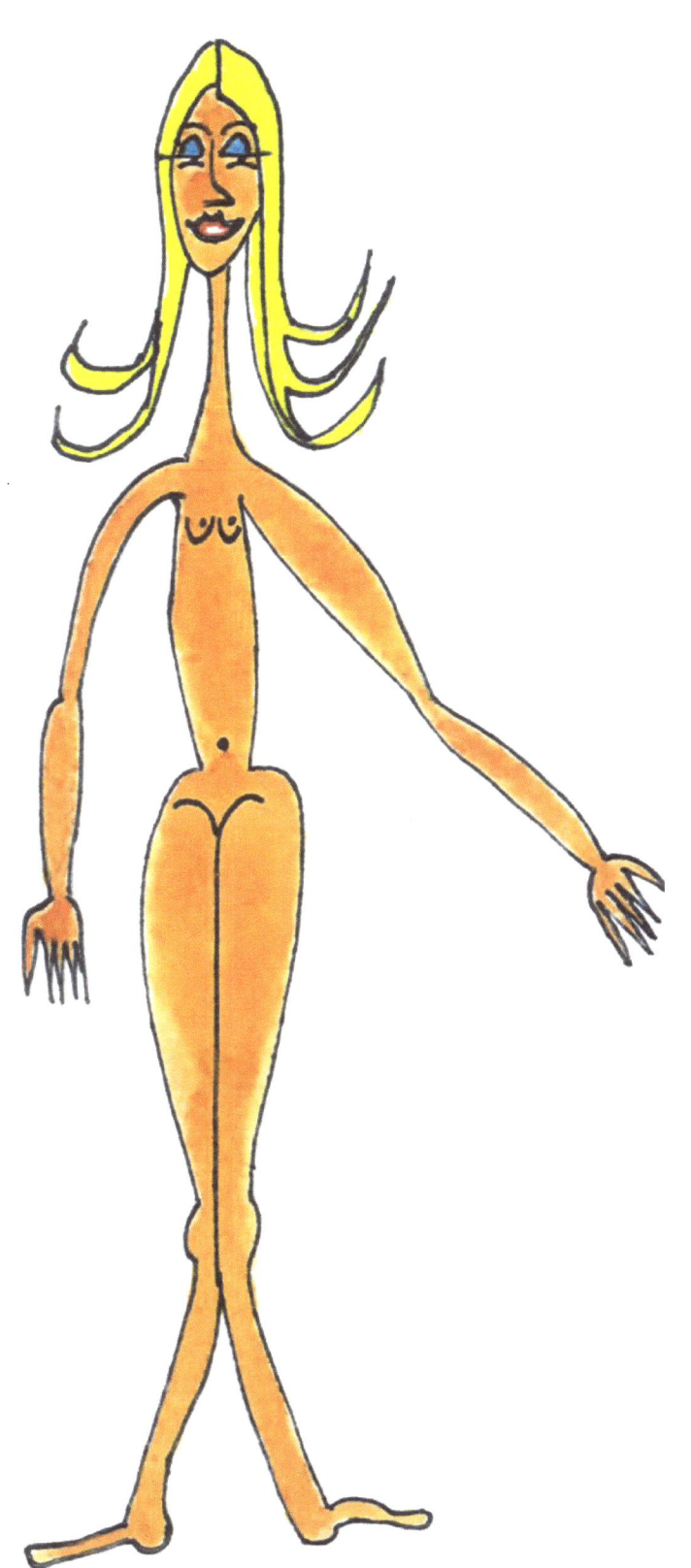

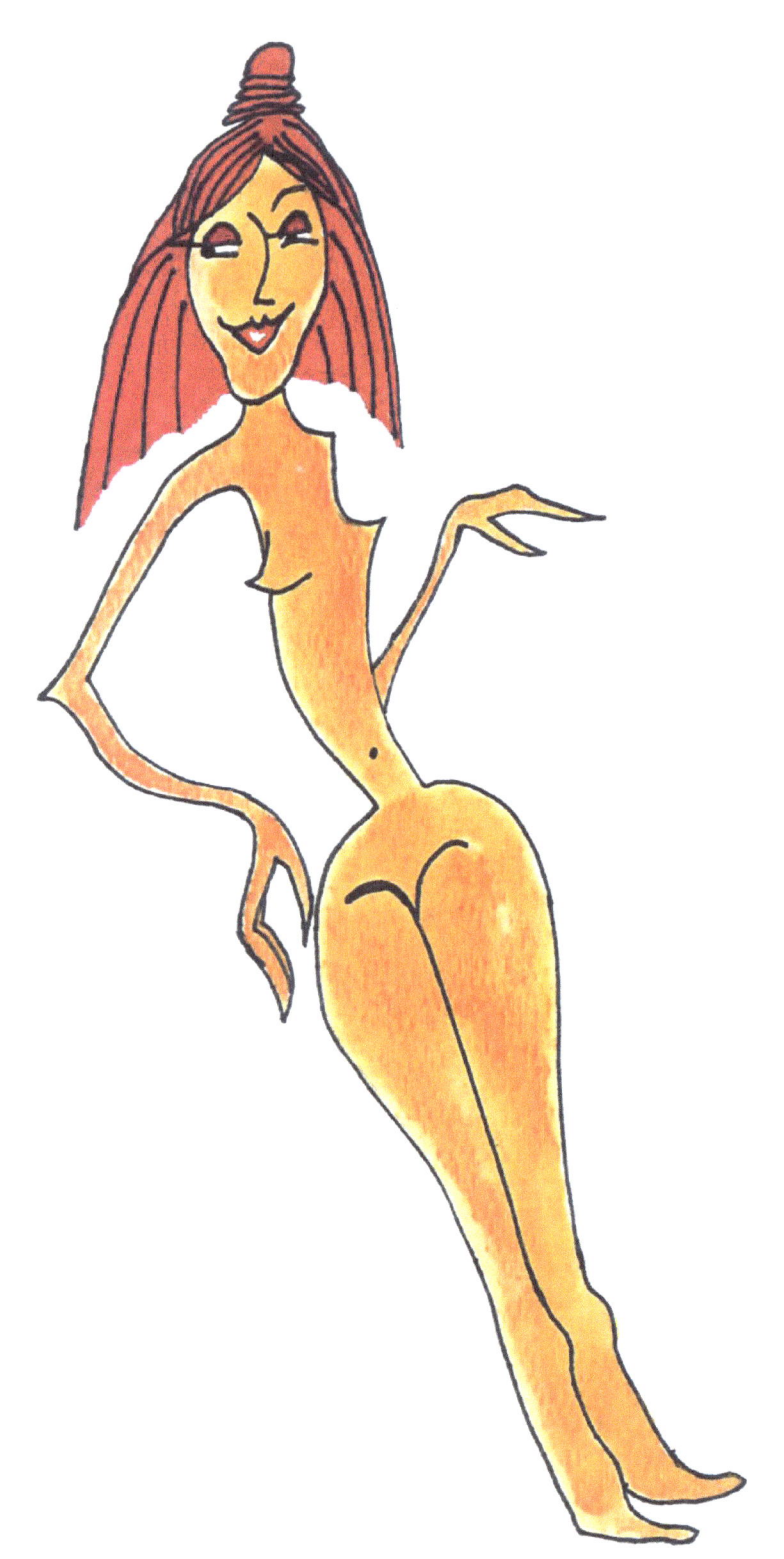

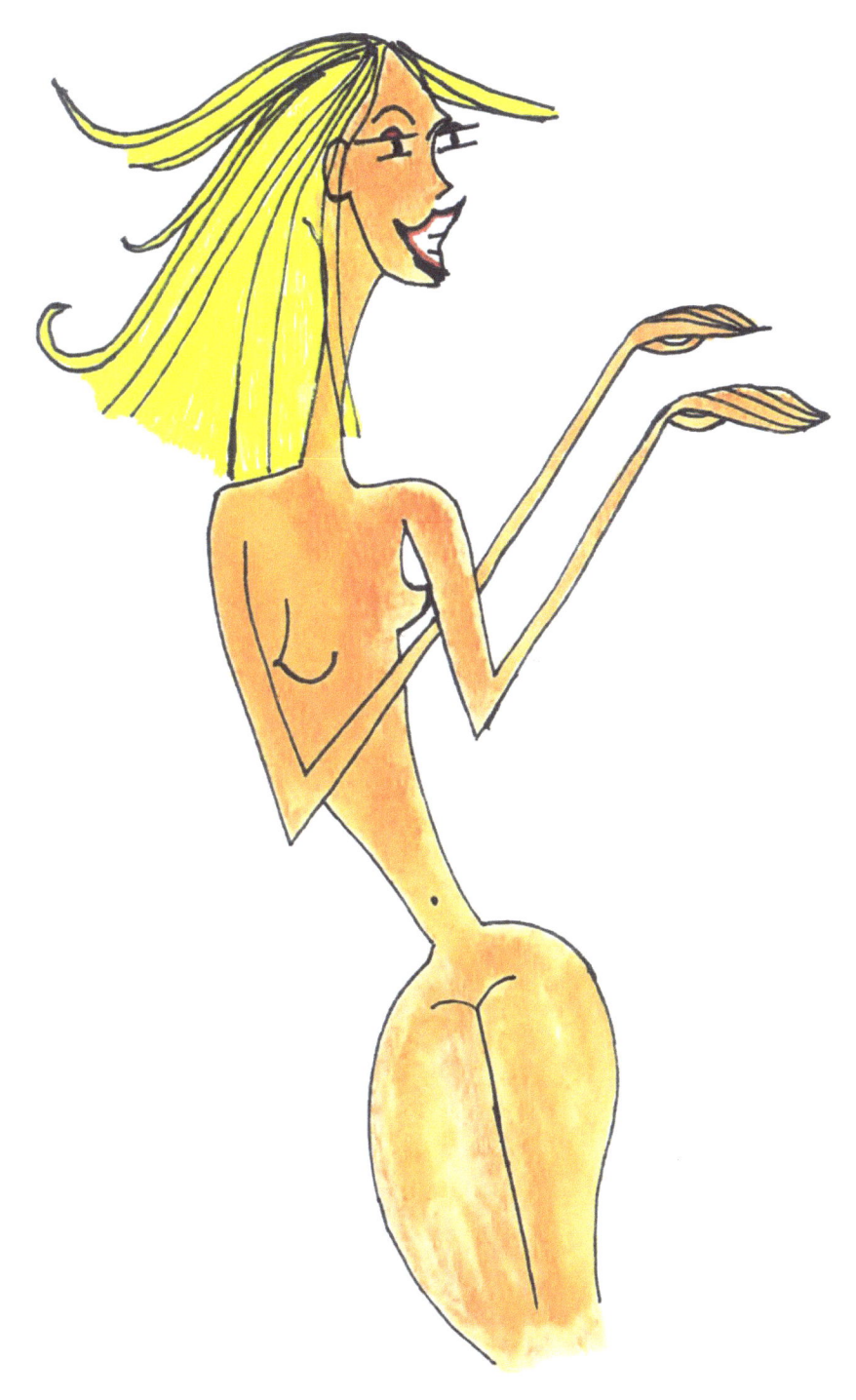

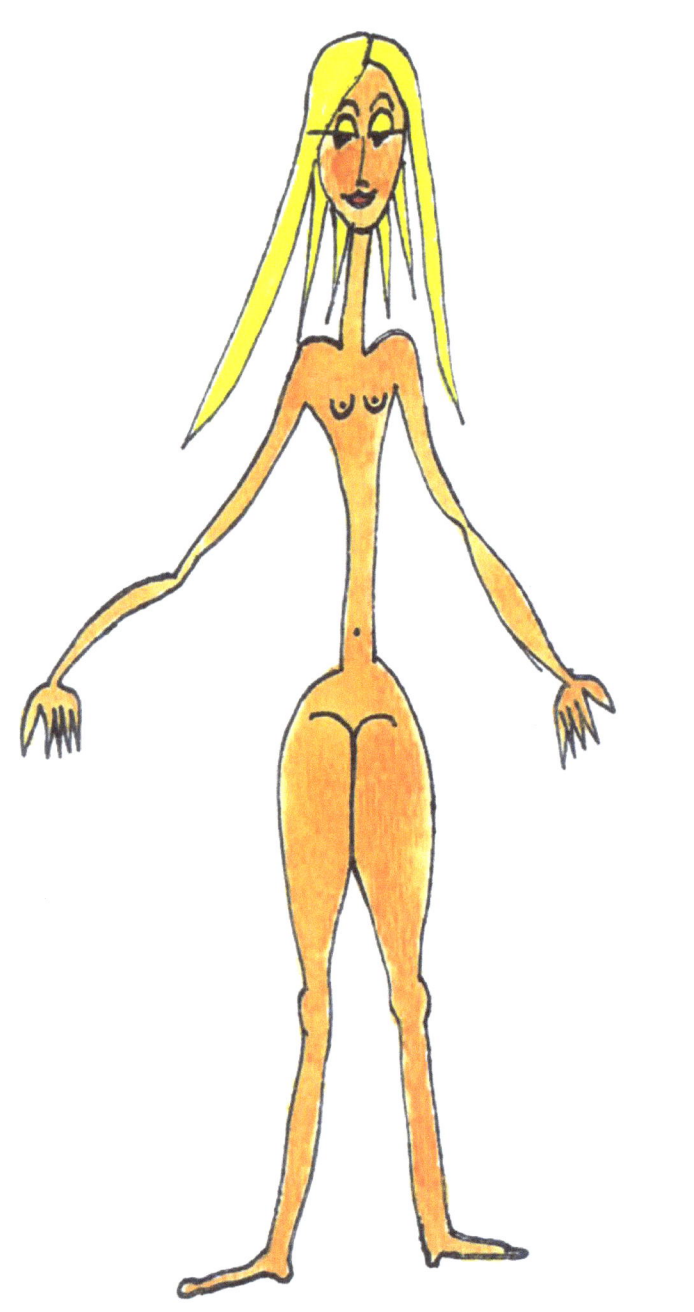

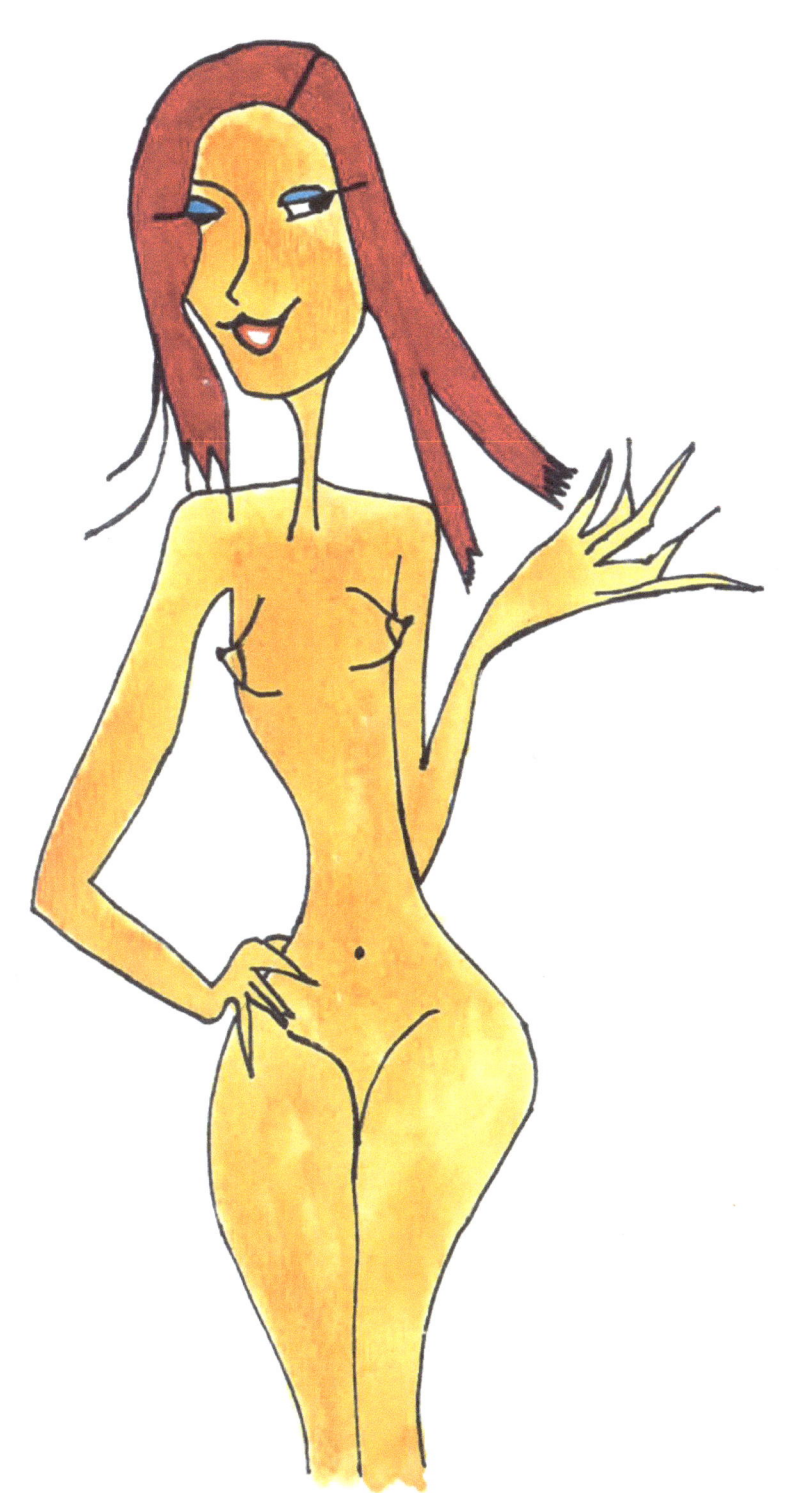

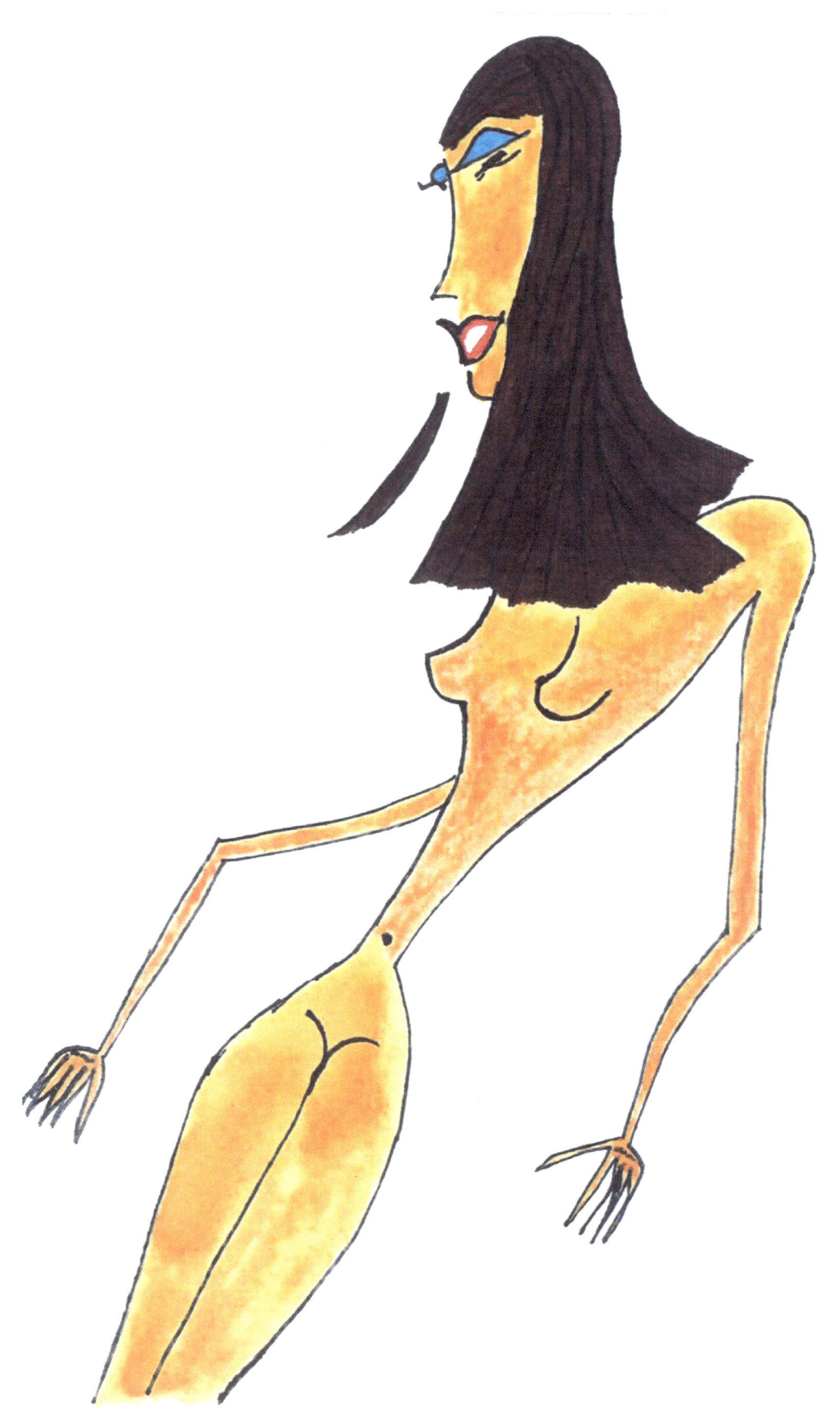

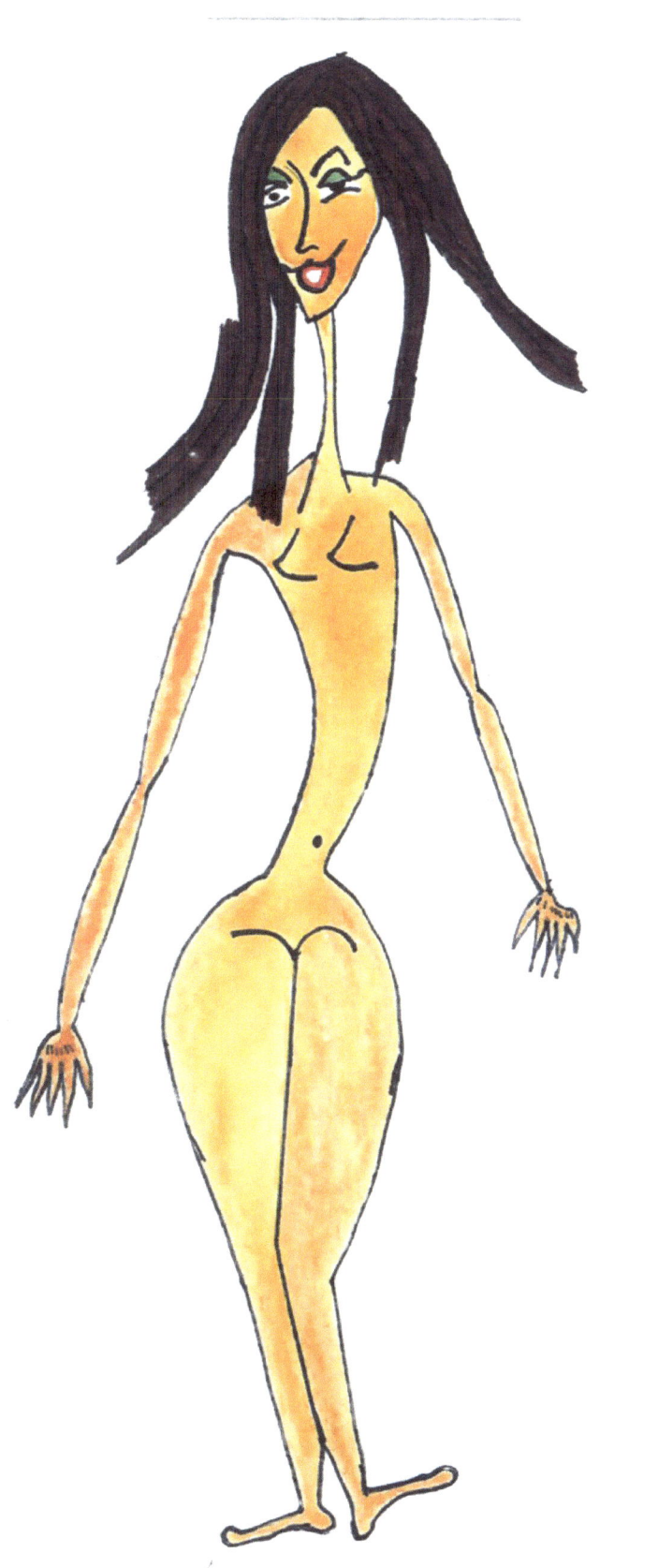

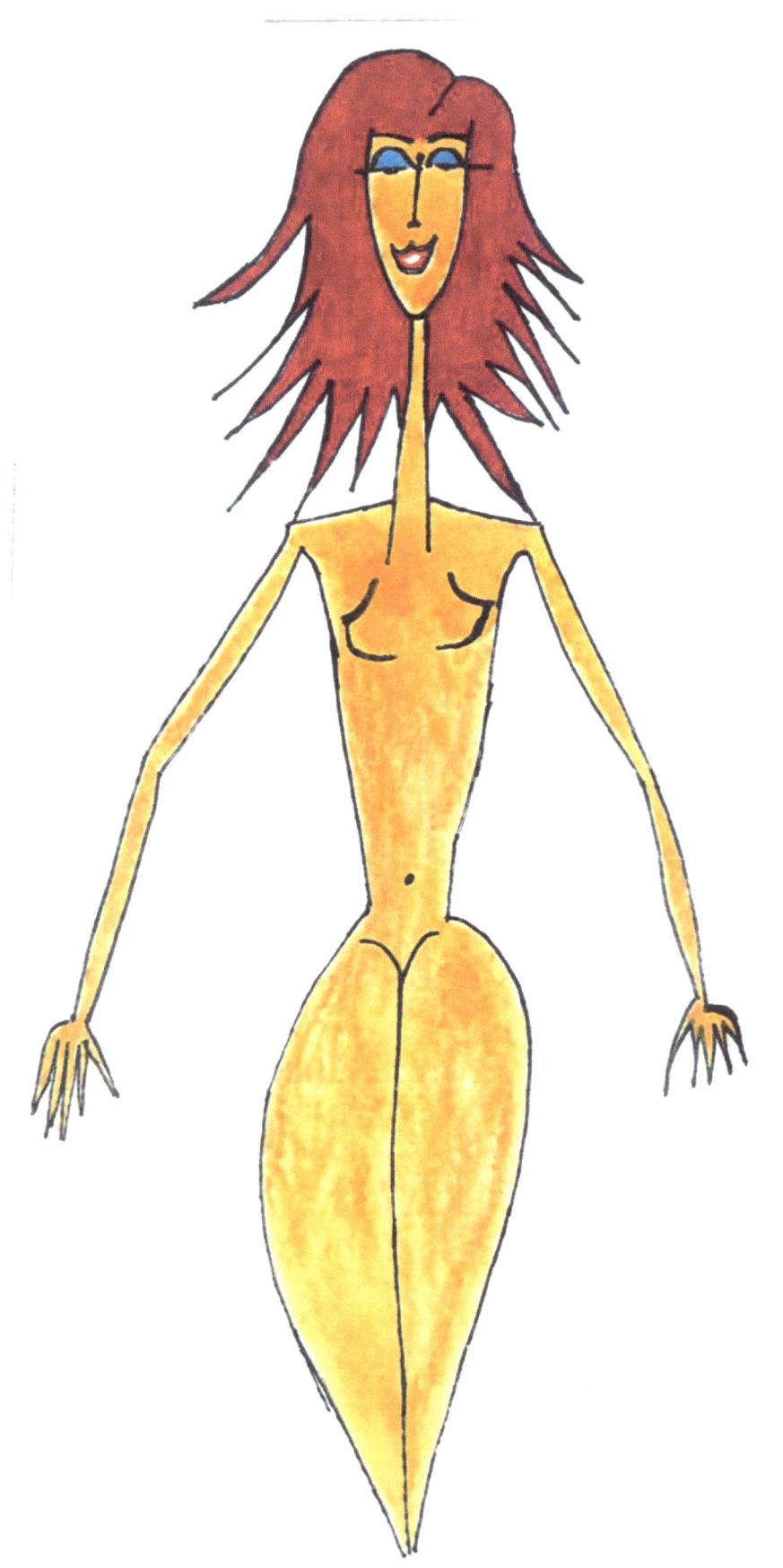

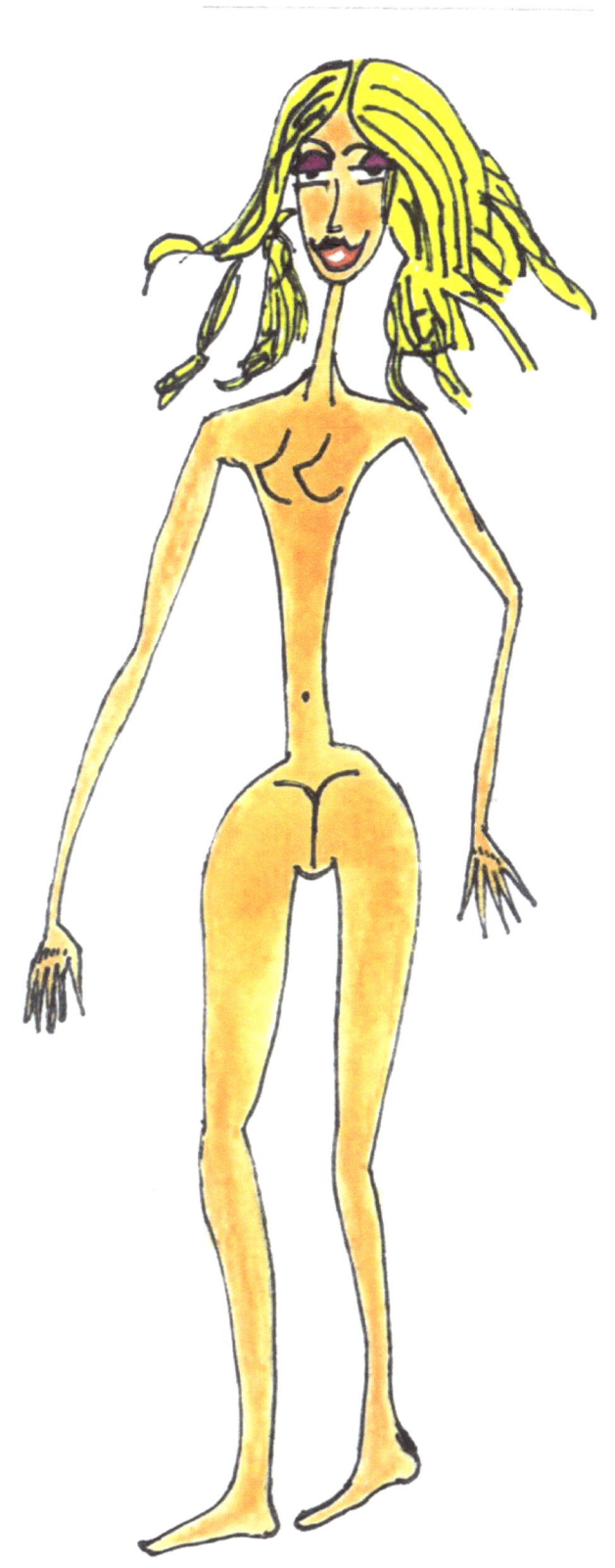

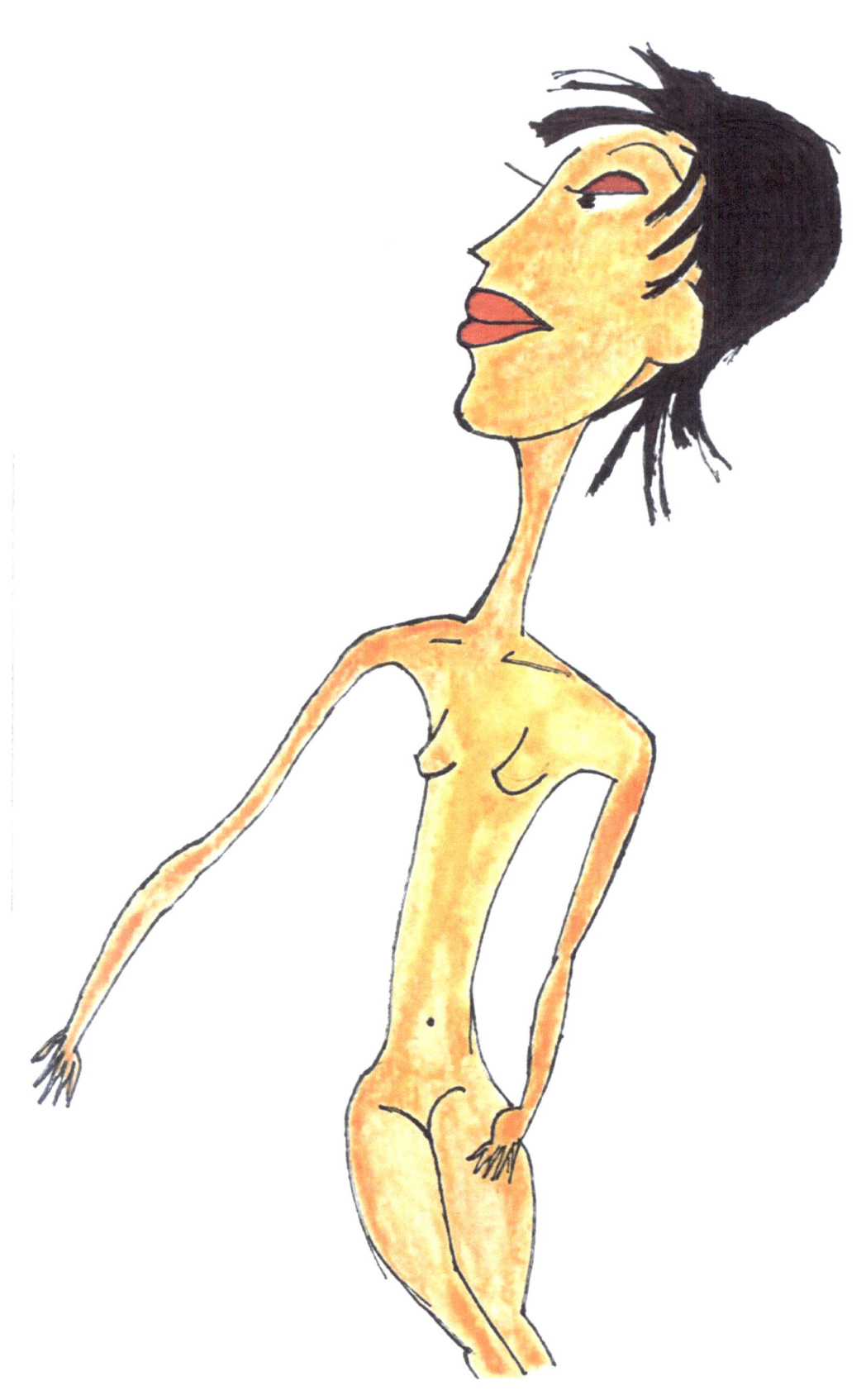

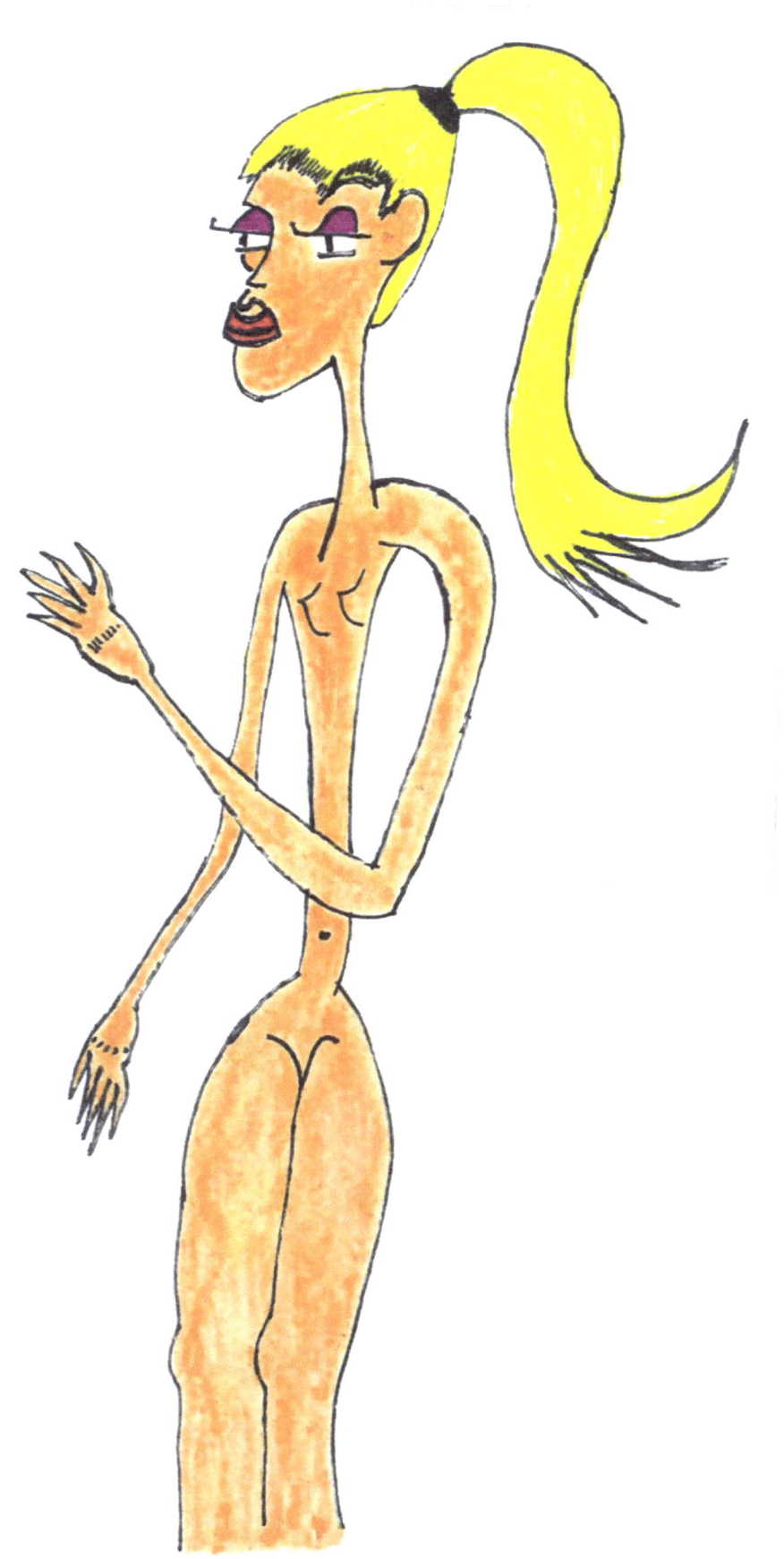

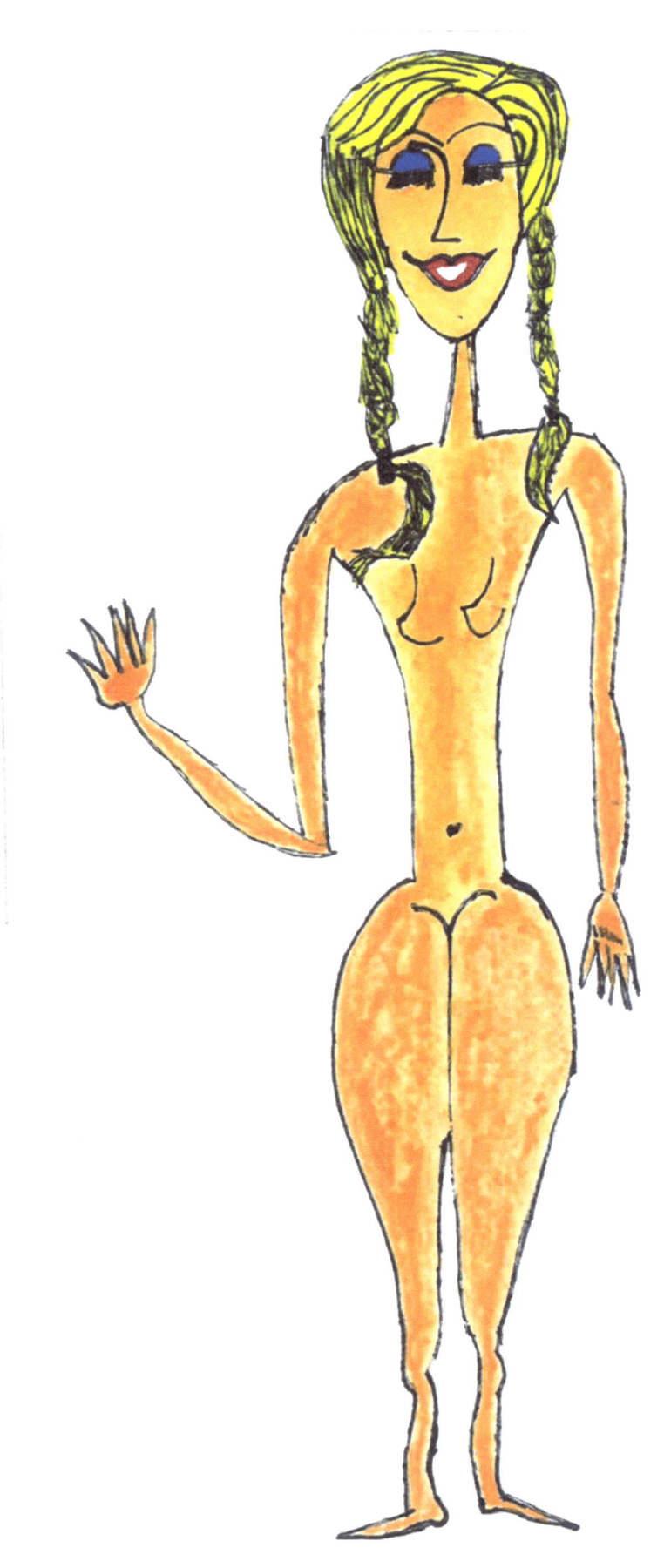

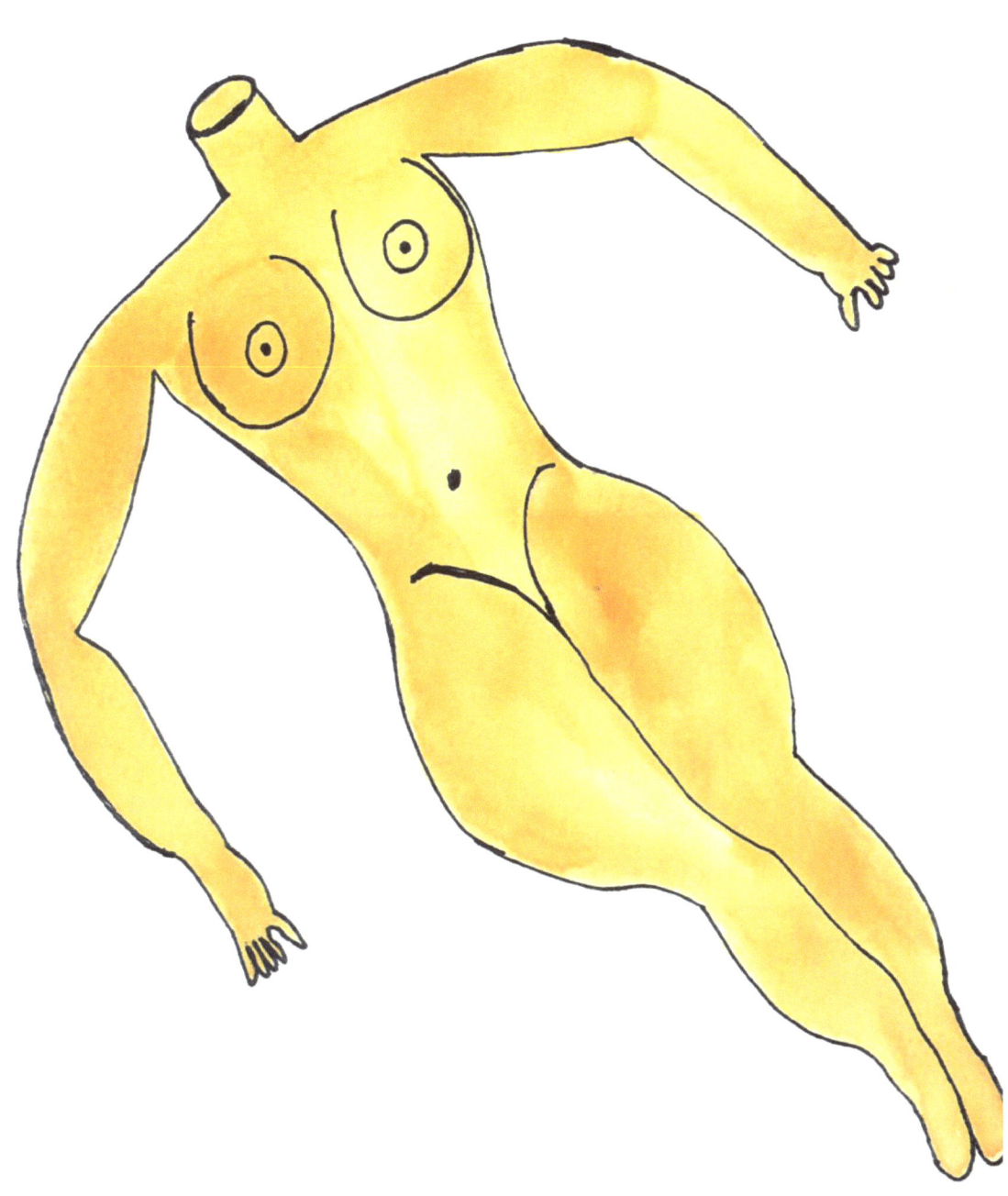

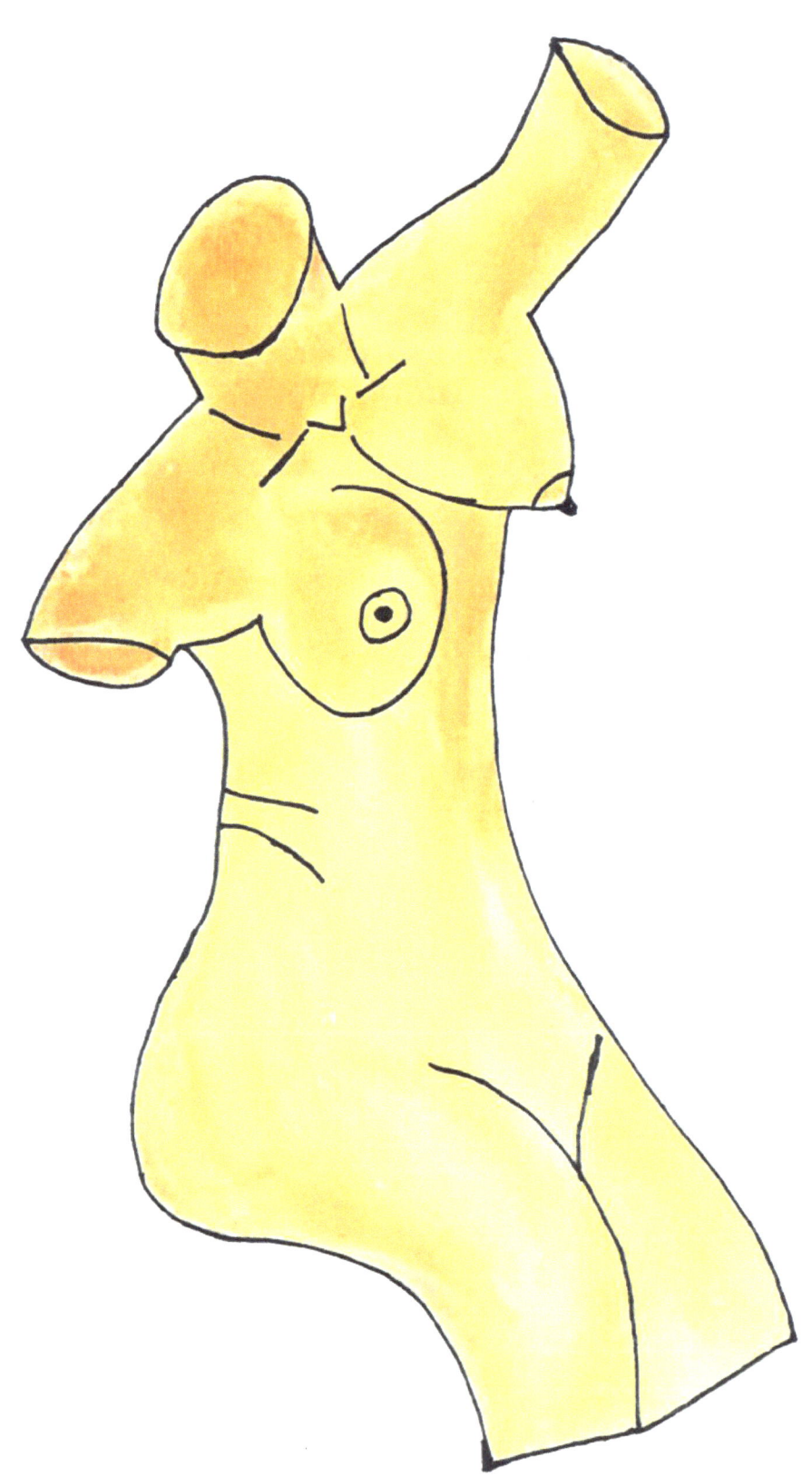

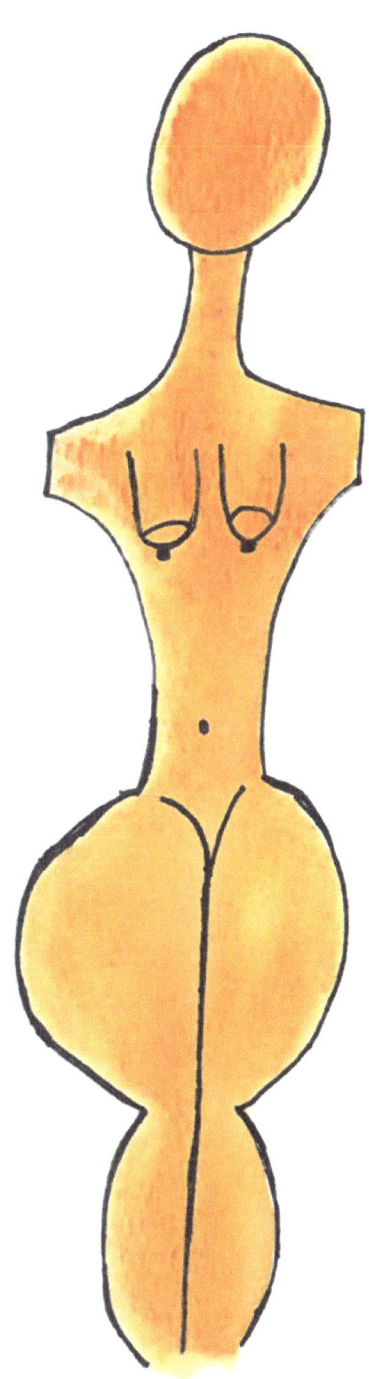

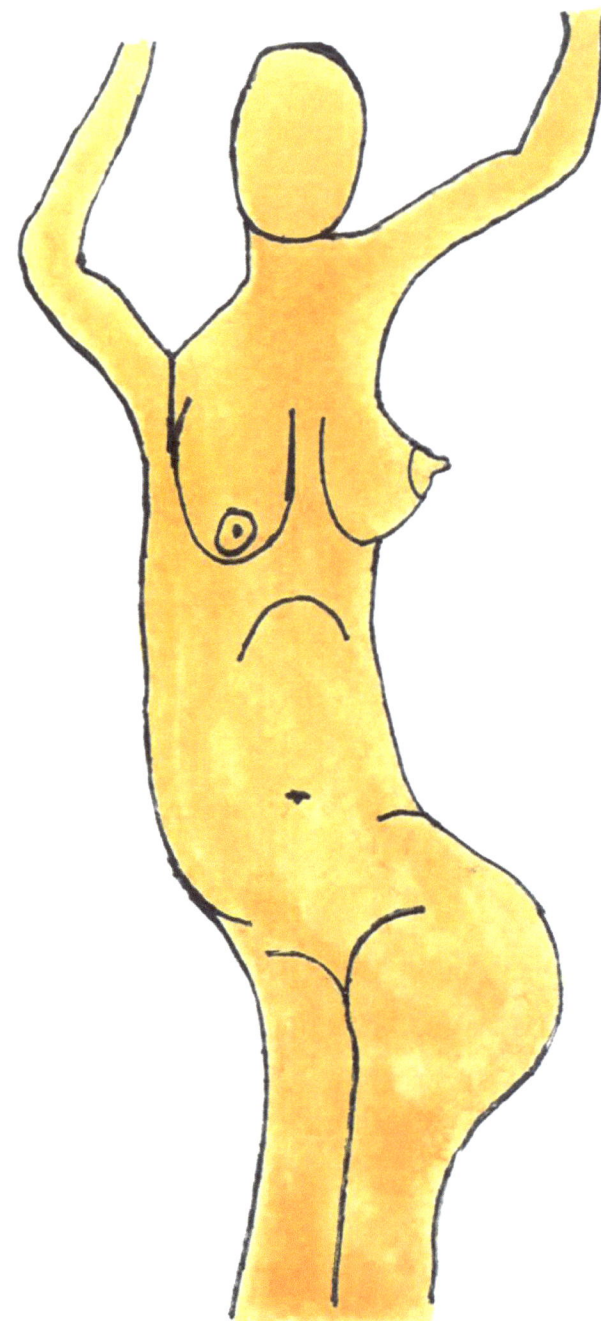

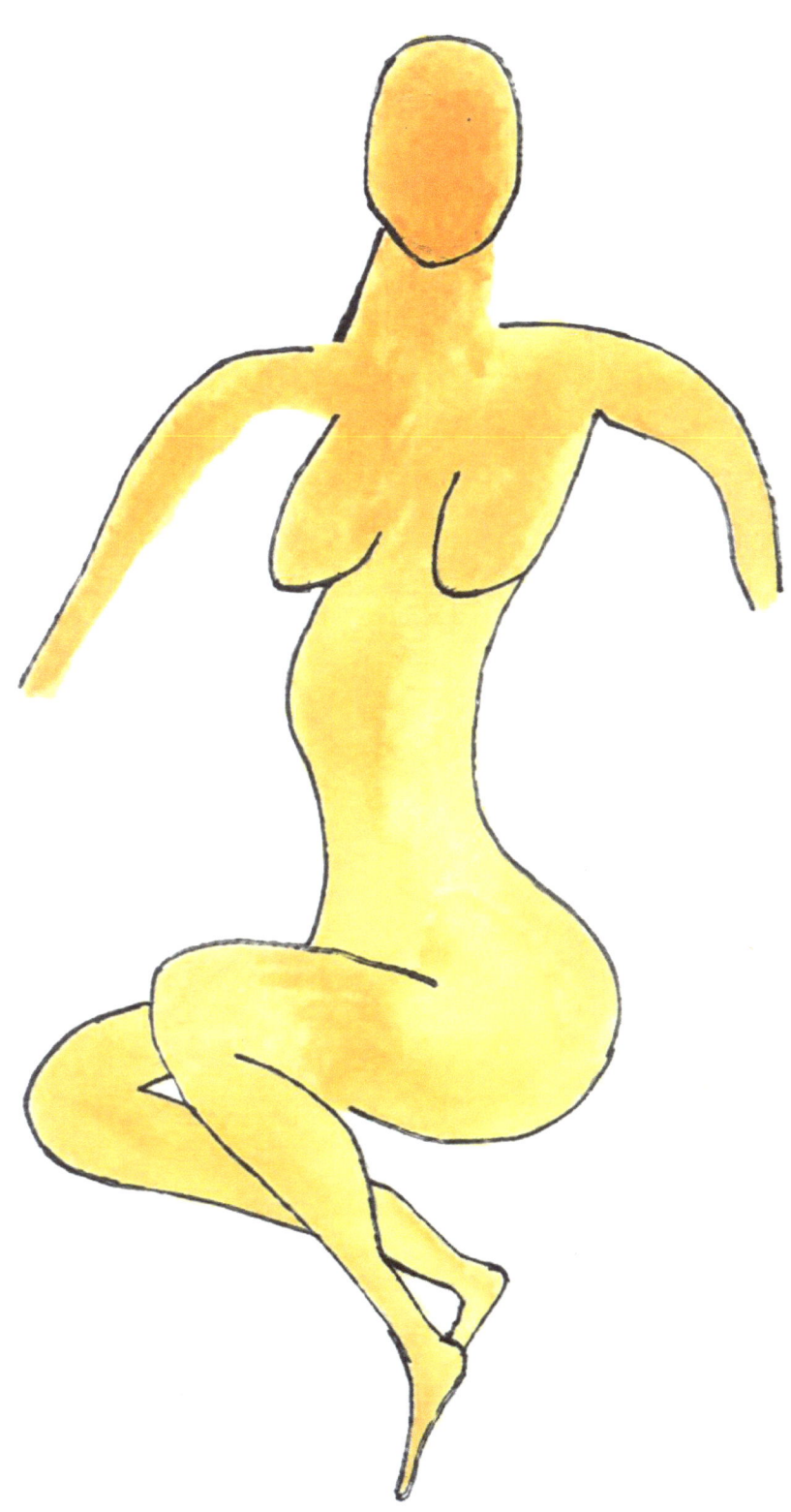

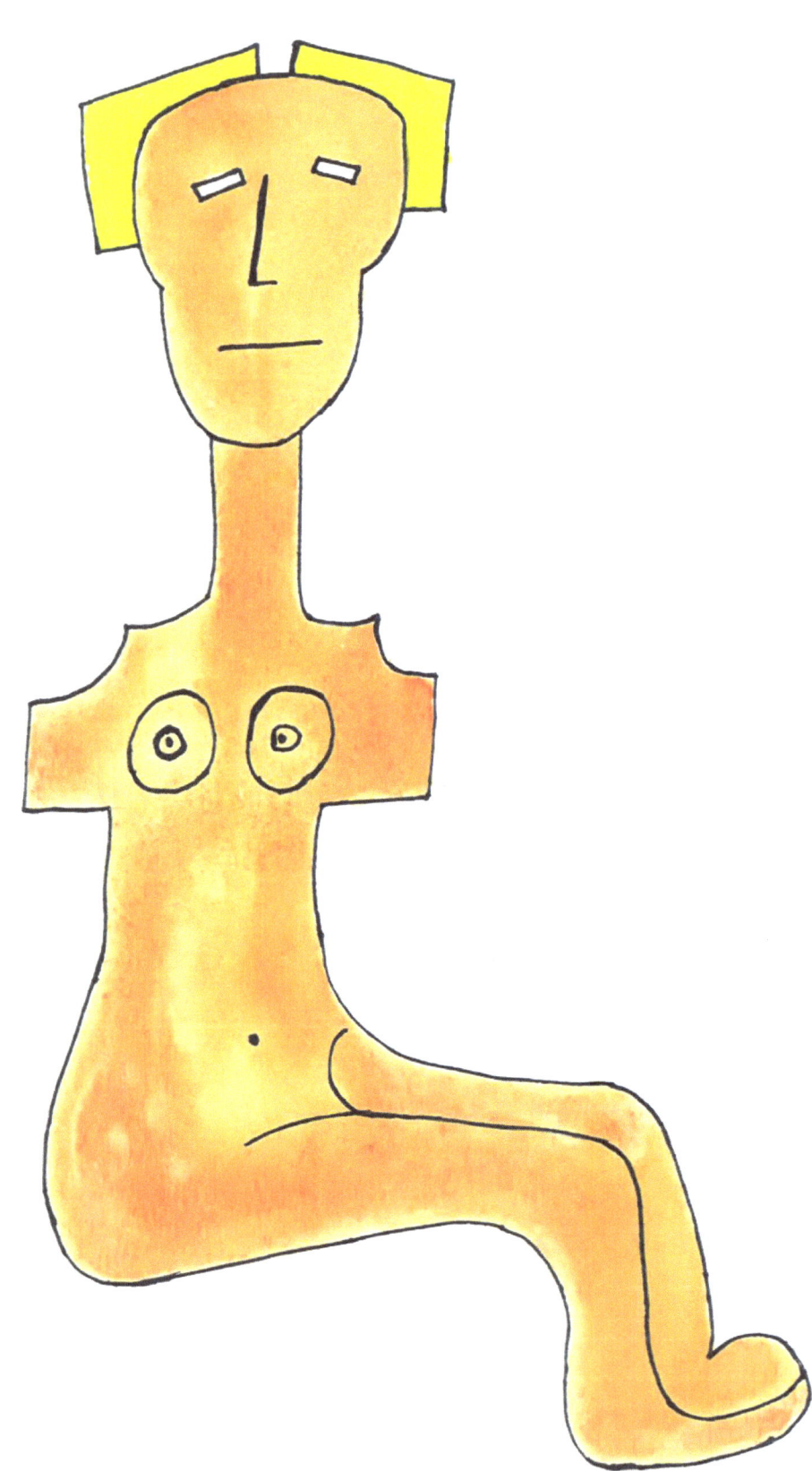

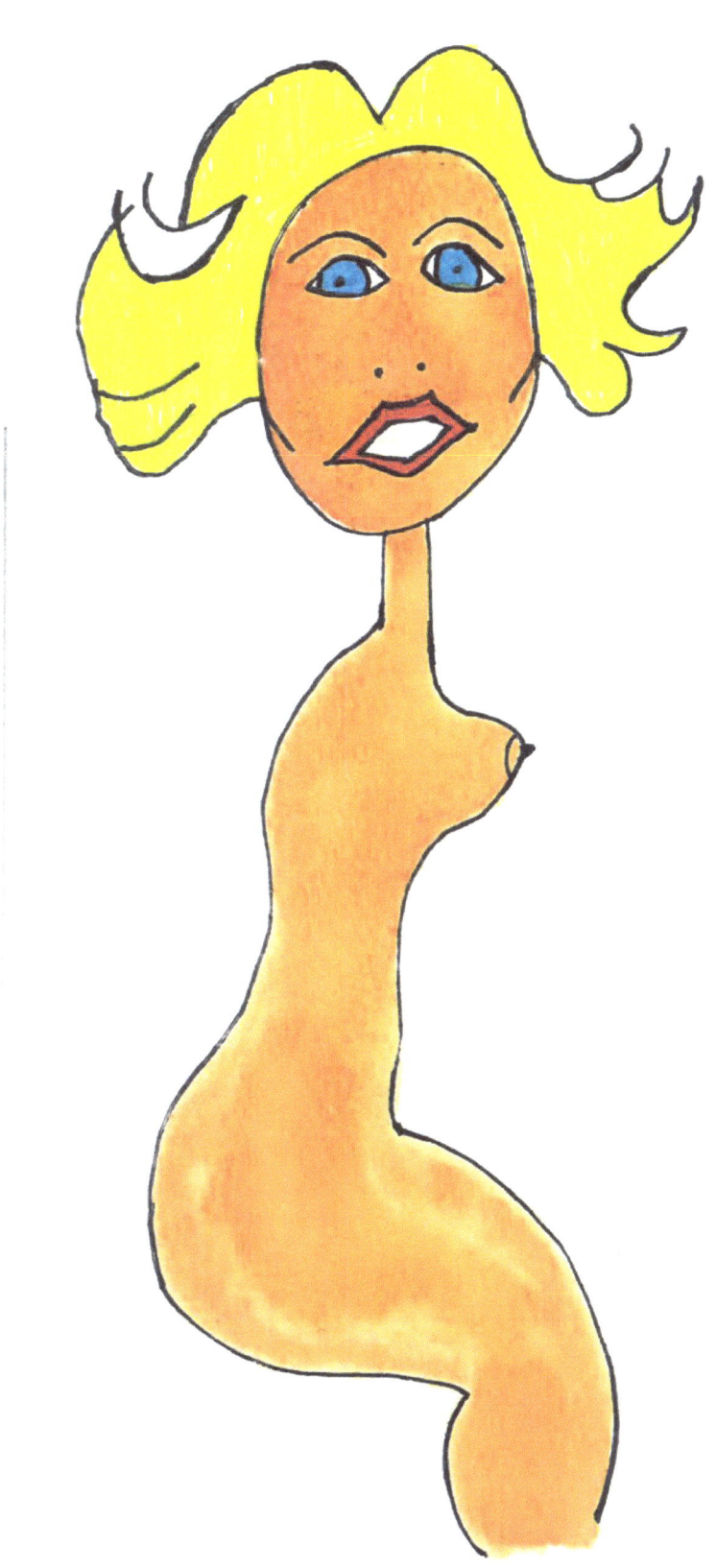

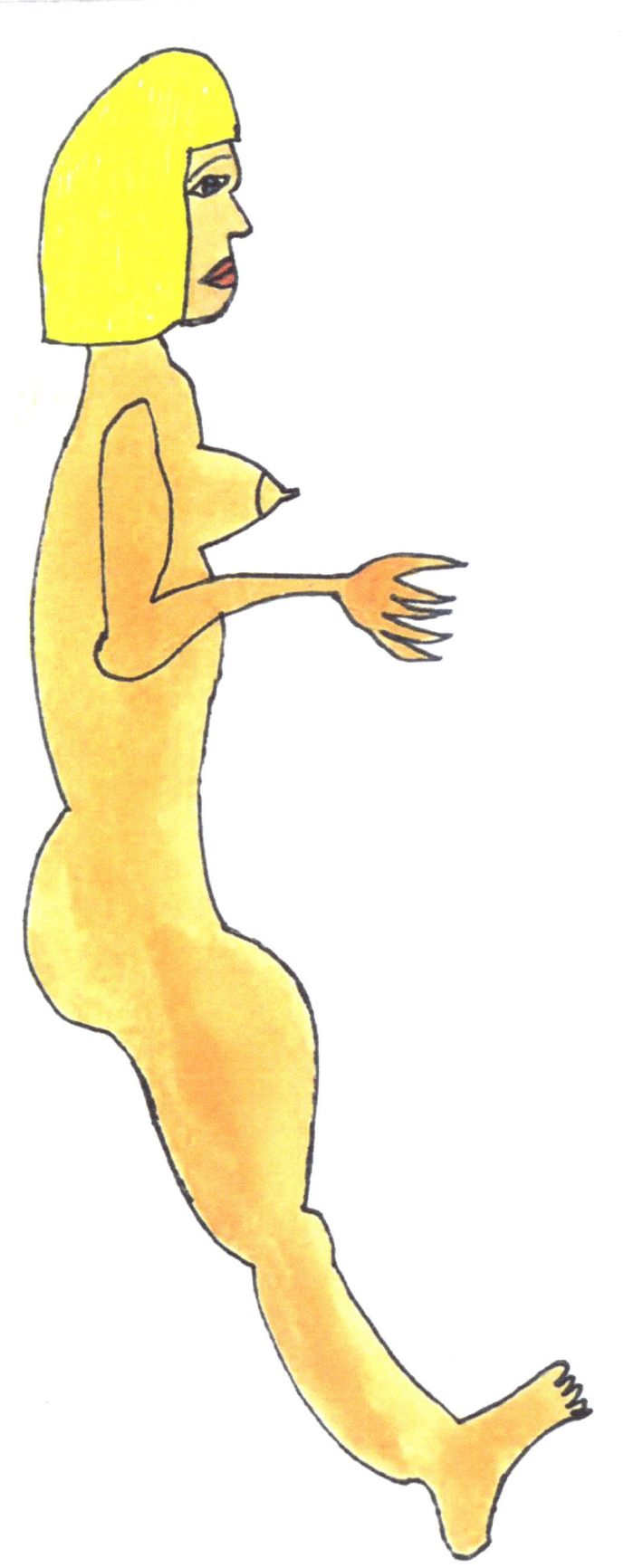

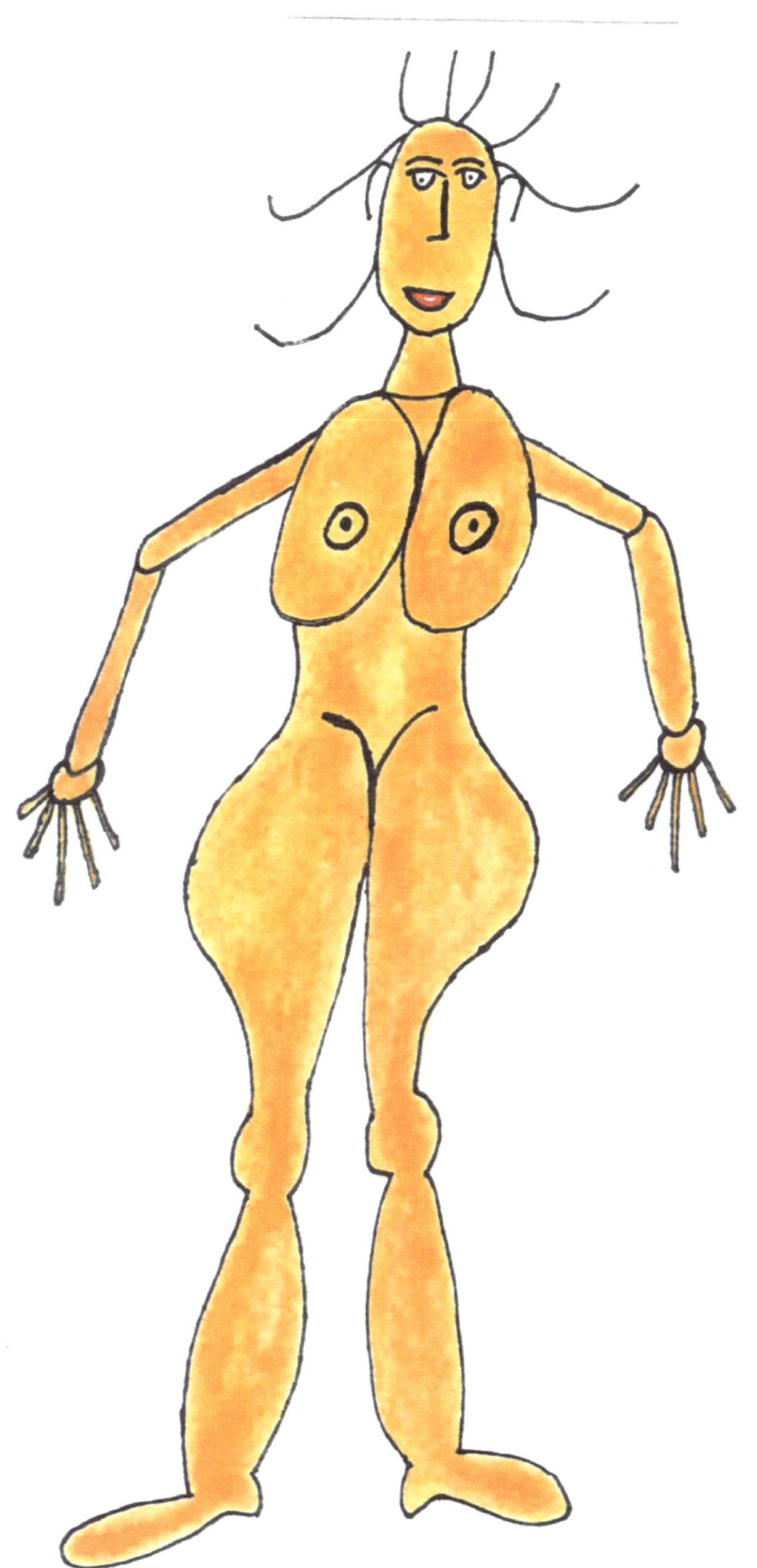

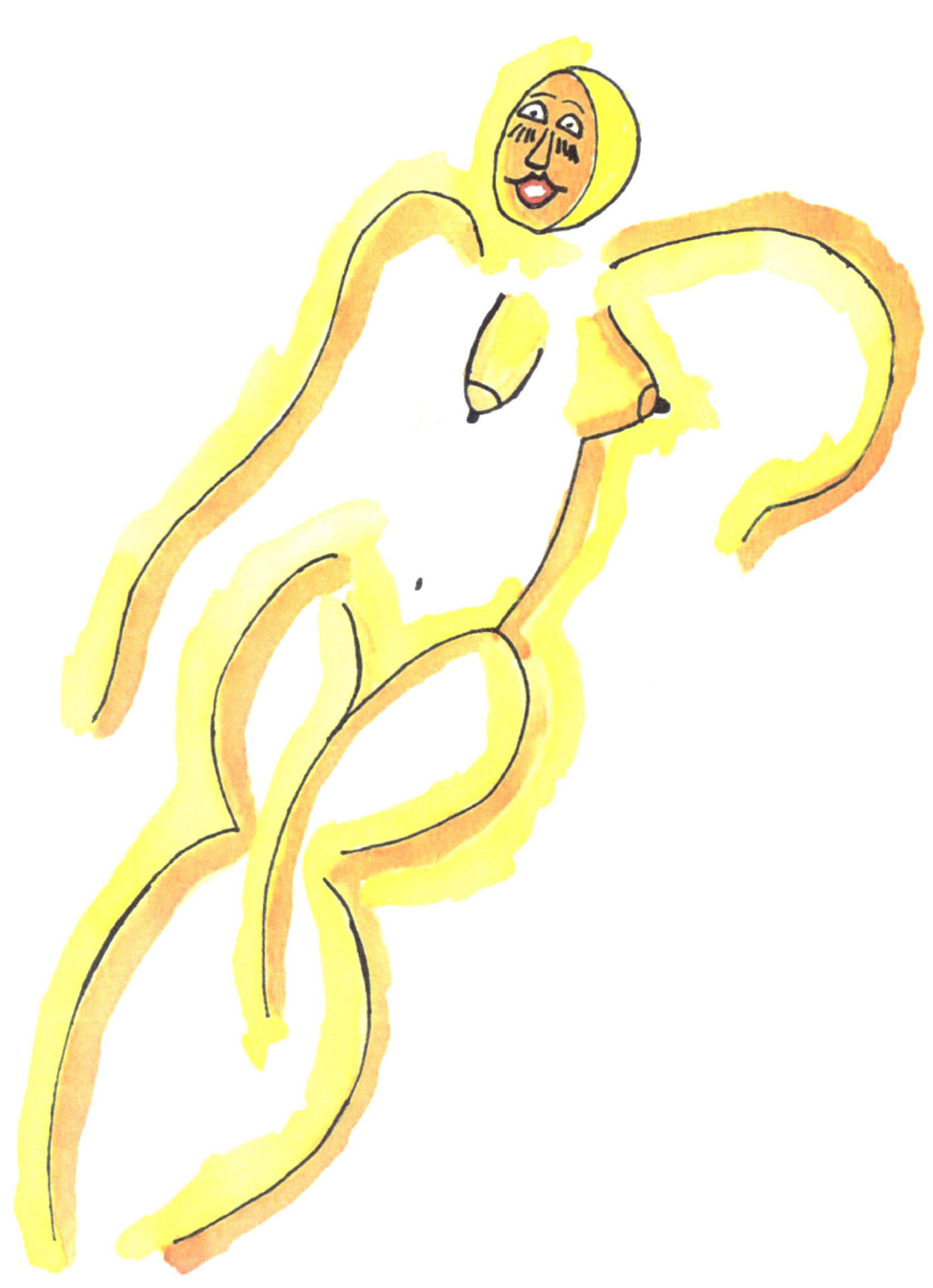

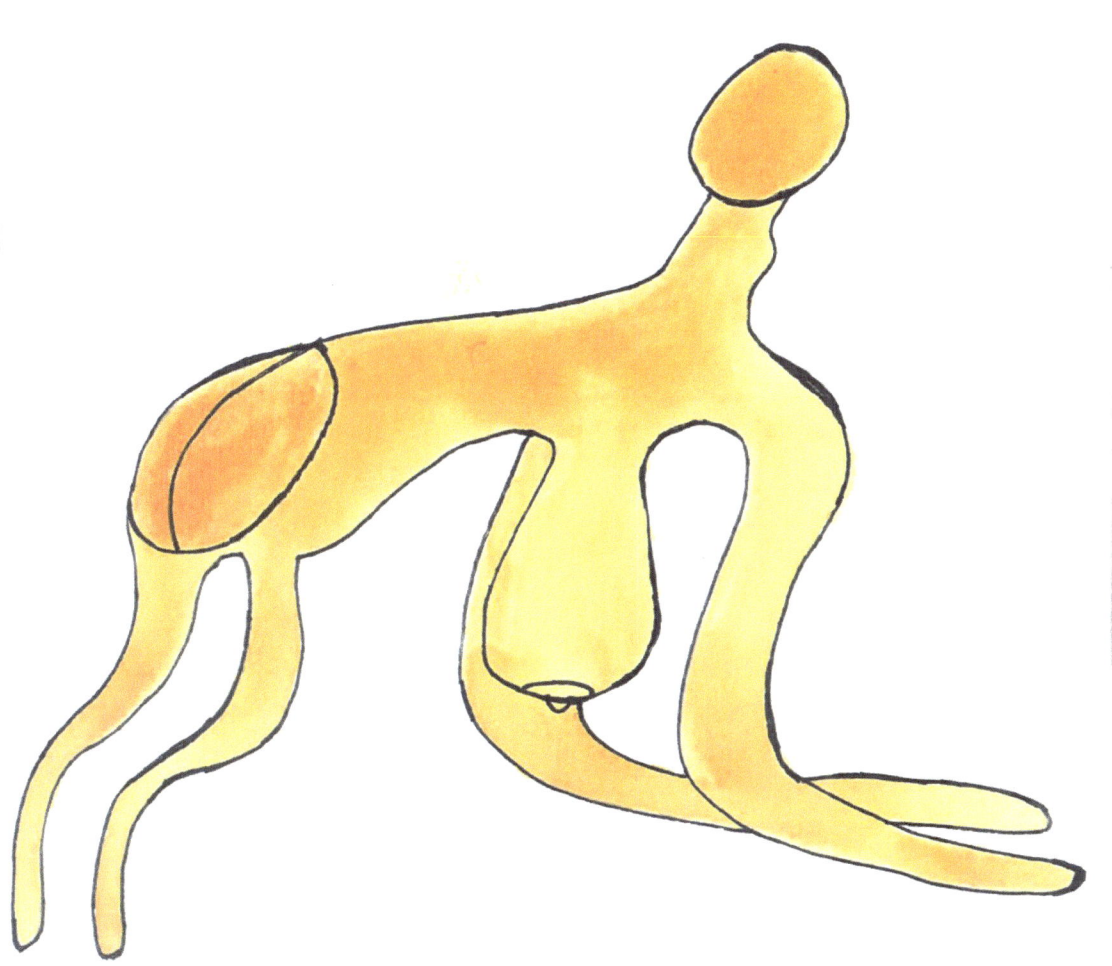

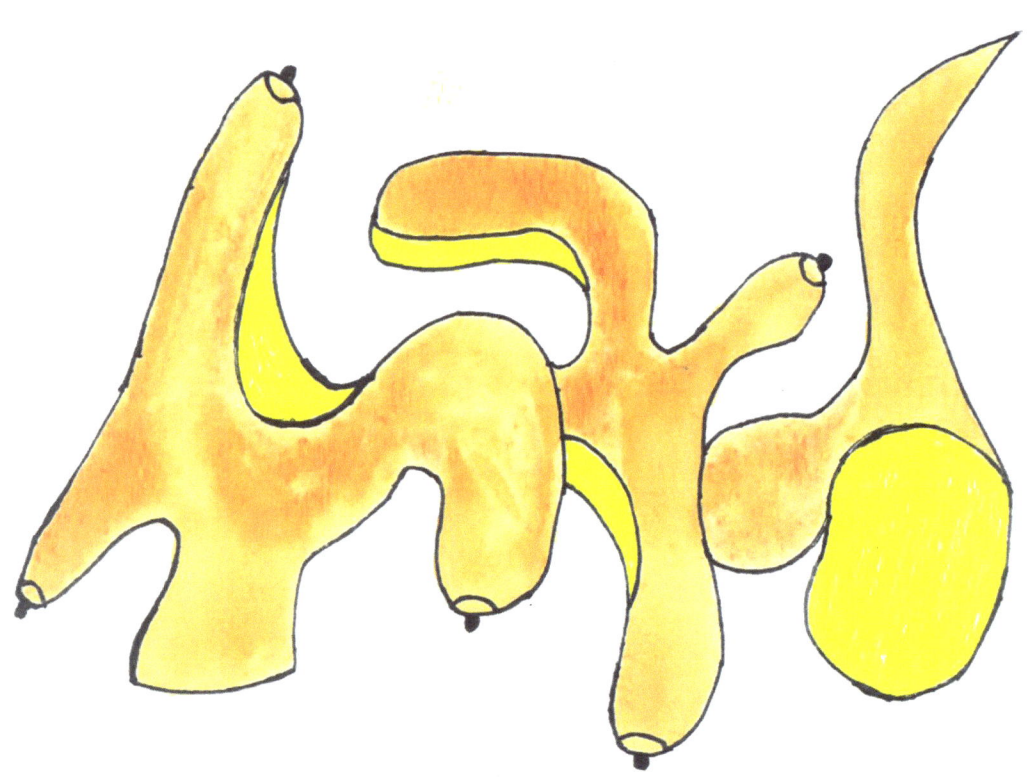

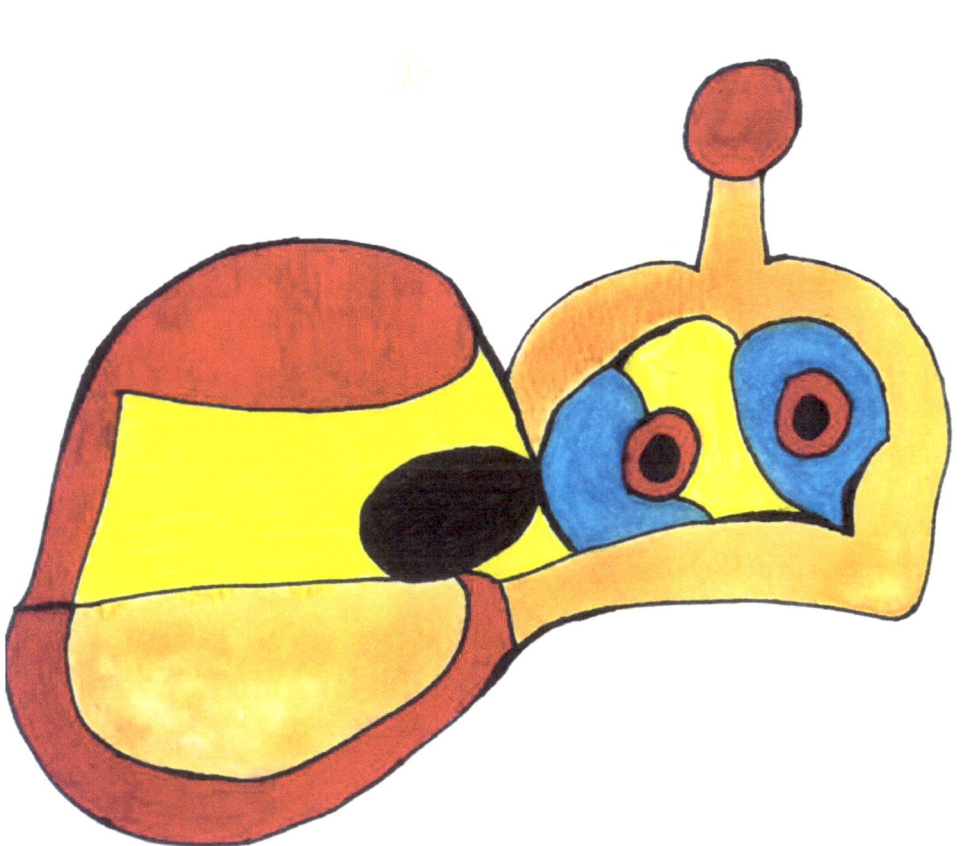

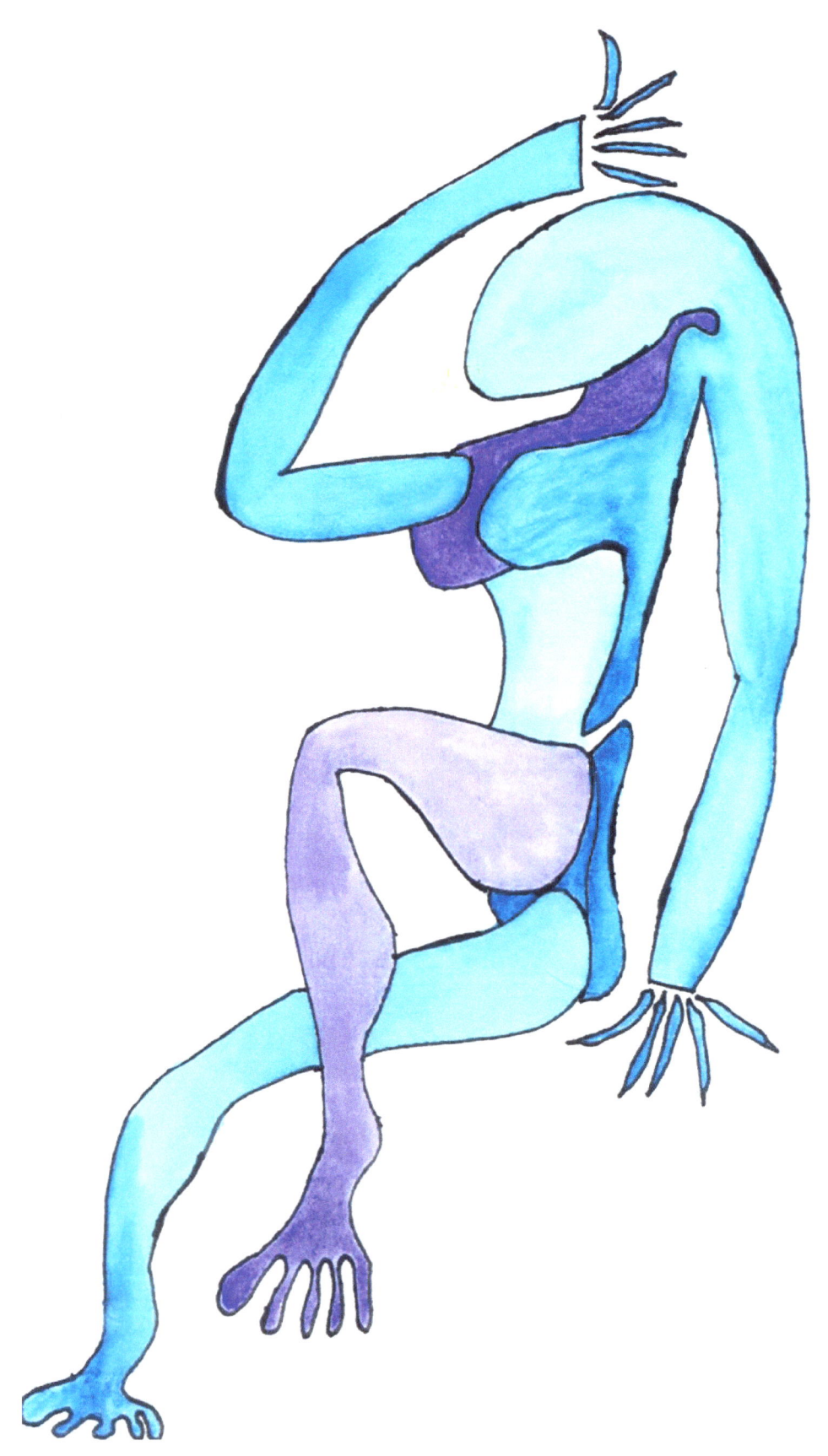

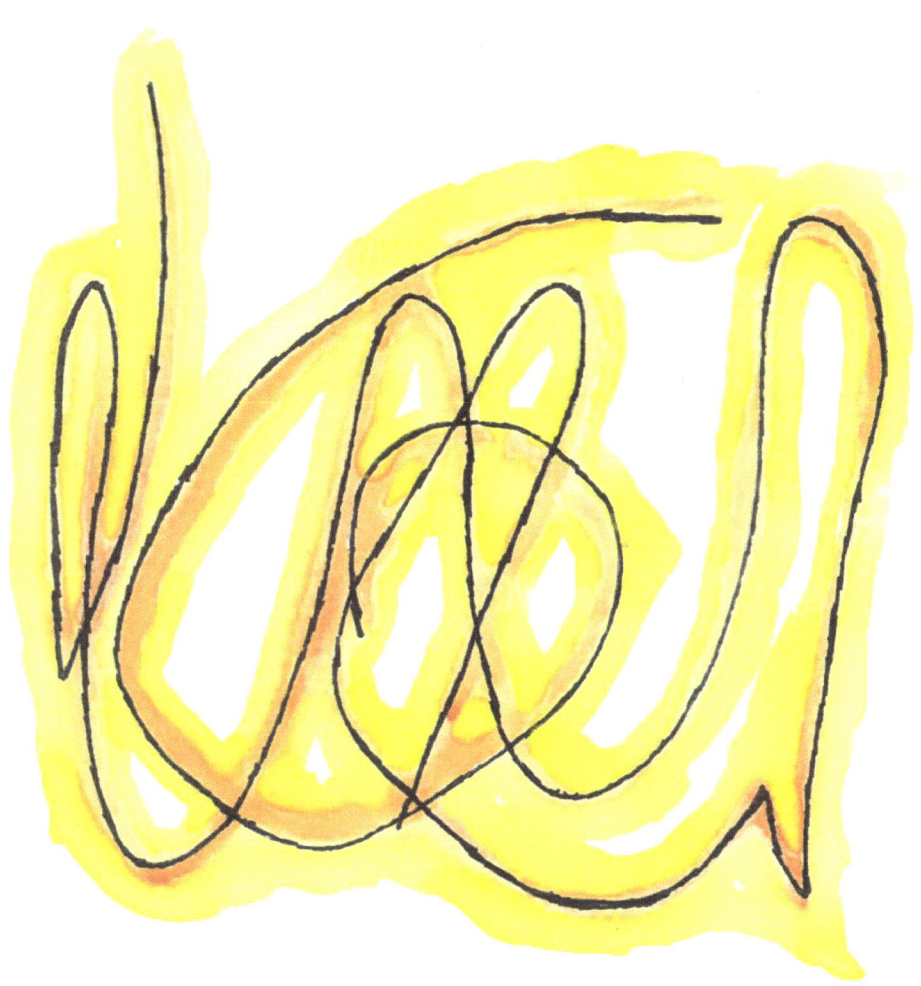

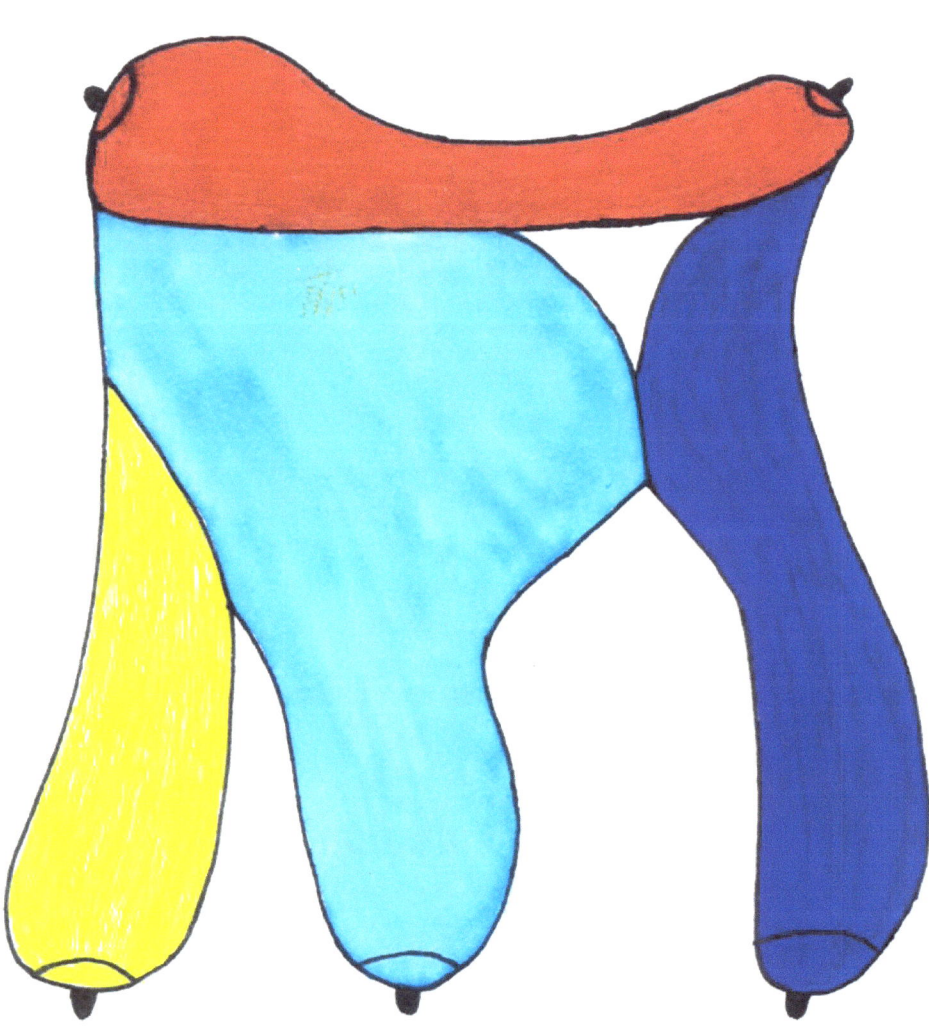

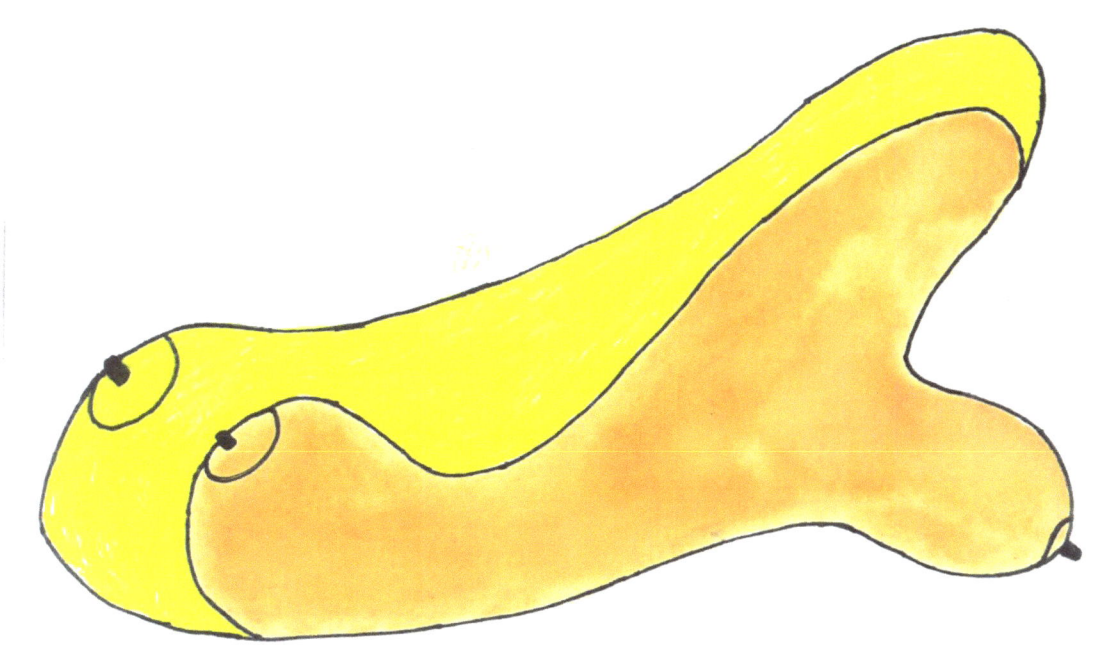

THE END